Advance Praise for
Renewing American Culture

"In a world filled with wonders—no matter the media's delight in featuring the pockets of chaos—let us applaud Scott T. Massey and Theodore Roosevelt Malloch for their positive vision for the future of the world."

Martha Ingram, Chairman of the Board, Ingram Industries

"As an American citizen of Latino descent, born and raised in this culture and raised by hardworking, God-fearing, dream-pursuing, emigrant parents, I find the waning understanding of the "core-values" of the American Experiment among the so-called "educated" masses of this generation to be alarming. I applaud Drs. Malloch and Massey for their deeply insightful analysis of our human need and their suggestions for re-establishing the pursuit of the uniquely American answer to that need."

**Jim Ortiz, Pastor: My Friend's House and
President, Latino Coalition for Faith & Community Initiatives**

"A magnificently old fashioned book that offers a fresh and absolutely appropriate guide for living in the new global age."

**Rodney Stark, author of *The Victory of Reason:
How Christianity Led to Freedom, Capitalism, and Western Success***

"In this invigorating book the authors show that the pursuit of happiness has been the core American value, and one that continues to provide a shared moral and spiritual foundation to the American people. The pursuit of happiness is as real a goal for Americans today as it was for the Founders, and humane education is the key to it."

**Roger Scruton, author of
The Meaning of Conservatism and *Modern Philosophy***

"At a time when our nation cries for an affirmation of shared cultural values the authors provide us with this book a compelling occasion to engage with ideas that matter and explore the values that define us as Americans."

**Michael Sartisky, President,
Louisiana Endowment for the Humanities**

"Theodore Roosevelt Malloch and Scott T. Massey are not embarrassed to consider the question of values, and are not afraid to propose humanist values as normative. This is therefore an original work, and an important one. "

**Edward N. Luttwak, Senior Fellow,
Center for Strategic and International Studies and
Author of *Strategy: the Logic of War and Peace***

"Turbulent times, complex trends, quick fixes, and barked sound-bites do not make a happy combination, and so we are very fortunate to have Ted Malloch and Scott Massey on the case. *Renewing American Culture* is not something that can be done with the ease of flipping a light switch, but requires us all to draw fresh insight and strength from our foundational documents, principles and ideals. Their remarkable book helps lead the way."

Stephen Klimczuk, Principal, A.T. Kearney and
Former Director, World Economic Forum

"Here, for the first time under one roof, is a serious and provocative consideration of the relationship between human capital, social capital, and spiritual capital. This is a cutting edge commentary on the necessary and sufficient conditions for the pursuit of happiness in the twenty-first century".

Gordon Lloyd,
Professor of Public Policy, Pepperdine University

"It is one of the virtues of *Renewing American Culture: the Pursuit of Happiness* that it places the humanities within our history, our virtues, and our lack of virtues. It is another that it places its discussion within the international currents of our world. And, finally, it suggests how we should respond and act."

Paul Marshall, Senior Fellow,
Freedom House's Center for Religious Freedom

"The pursuit of happiness enlivens the prospect of American possibility, and as this book demonstrates, the future is, indeed, bright!"

D. Michael Lindsay,
Professor of Sociology, Princeton University

"There's a debate about the future of America. In the long term I'm a pessimist, but I have never seen the case for optimism put better than in 'The Pursuit of Happiness'."

Digby Anderson,
Founder of The Social Affairs Unit, London

"Malloch and Massey appeal to America's soul to reject "happiness" as "selfish pleasure" and to honor it anew as an inalienable human "right" and a revolutionary, civic "obligation". How blessed are those who heed this truth!"

Christopher Hancock,
Former Dean of Bradford Cathedral and Oxford University

"As a venture capitalist, I believe that the concept of the pursuit of happiness and spiritual capital are essential for the economy, for business, culture, and the future of our families. This is great stuff."

Tom Zucosky, Chief Investment Officer,
Discovery Capital, New York

"The intelligent optimism—and boundless verve—of Drs. Massey and Malloch allows these pages to transcend academic debates and enter the sphere of humanistic philosophy. Their vision of a renewed culture and a new humanities encompasses all professions, all needs, all beliefs."

Scott Noppe-Brandon,
Executive Director, Lincoln Center Institute

"Drs. Malloch and Massey succeed where so many have fallen short: in clear and certain terms they delineate the essential role that the humanities play in our lives and argue that it is through the humanities that we can renew both ourselves and our national culture. Bravo!"

Stanley Romanstein, President & CEO,
Minnesota Humanities Commission

"First, Luther's 95 Theses. Now, Malloch and Massey's 36 Propositions. At stake? A 21st century reformation of America—a deep cultural renewal of its core values—that will offer to future generations profound hope and guarantee the continued pursuit of happiness."

Robert Hamrin,
Founder and President, Great Dads

"In reaching back to America's religious and intellectual well springs and relating these to the contemporary challenges of politics, commerce and the academy through the unifying concept of spiritual capital, Malloch and Massey have made a defining contribution to substantive reflection about the underlying factors that make any culture or civilization lasting and significant.'

Justin D Cooper,
President of Redeemer University College, Canada

"Historically, great societies all come to crossroads where the choices that will determine both the moral character of their people and ultimately the strength of their nation must be made. Scott Massey and Theodore Malloch rightly perceive that America is at just such a place of crisis and opportunity, and their vision for our moral and intellectual renewal is comprehensive and compelling."

The Very Rev. Kenneth Swanson, Ph.D.,
Dean and Rector, Christ Church Cathedral, Nashville, Tennessee

For our children—Alec, Cameron,
        Ian, Morgan, Nigel, and Trevor—
future leaders, and
generations of leaders to come

Renewing American Culture

The Pursuit of Happiness

**Theodore Roosevelt Malloch
and Scott T. Massey**

M&M Scrivener Press

Published by   M & M Scrivener Press
72 Endicott Street, Salem, MA 01970

http://www.mmscrivenerpress.com

Copyright © 2006 M & M Scrivener Press
First published 2006

10 9 8 7 6 5 4 3 2 1

Library of Congress Control Number: 2006922384

ISBN – 13: 978-0-9764041-1-8
ISBN – 10: 0-9764041-1-7

Conflicts and Trends™ in Business Ethics
Series Editor, Nicholas Capaldi

Front cover: *Sunrise, Jupiter Bay* by M. Kathryn Massey
http://www.masseyfineart.com

Printed in Canada on acid-free paper

Contents

Foreword

KEY FIGURES in America's political, corporate, and academic life have often brought to their leadership roles the breadth, depth of understanding, and qualities of judgment that came uniquely from the great traditions of the liberal arts and humanities. It is not so clear anymore that our culture or even our educational system, in particular, is now sustaining that tradition, which has nurtured public leadership in all three of these areas in the past.

Politically, Thomas Jefferson guided us into self governing independence by believing that the pursuit of truth was the highest form of his pursuit of happiness. This pursuit is inherently noncompetitive and communal. One person's discovery enriches another's search; the pursuit of truth helps keep us from the pursuit of each other. The great Jewish philosopher Franz Rosenzweig said that "truth is a noun only for God; for us it is only a verb." In the American tradition, it has been an active verb. Jefferson organized knowledge into three categories: memory, reason, and imagination. As a remembering, reasoning, and imagining people, we have become over the years more inclusive socially and more dynamic economically and culturally.

Jefferson gave us the ideal of a knowledge based democracy in which more people would have more access to more knowledge and the freedom to use it in more ways than in any other large country. Jefferson wanted to be remembered for founding a university rather than for being president of the United States. His ranging personal library provided the nucleus of the Library of Congress, which now contains 130 million items. His ideal inspired our program to put the primary documents of American history and culture on the Internet for young people everywhere, in the hope that reasoning and imagining will be encouraged by broader access to the memory we are in danger of losing.

Liberal learning based on memory and accountable to reason has also inspired corporate leaders, such as the late J. Irwin Miller, the former chairman of Cummins Engine. In "A Case for the Humanities" (Indianapolis: Indiana Humanities Council, 2000, p. 23), he said that:

> the humanities have something unique to say to a dehumanized society. They do not have to lecture the young or try to impose an ideology . . . rather, it seems to me that their timeless beauty is to let both the best and worst of our past speak in ways that will truly be heard. The humanities can hold up before us the best that humans accomplished over the centuries—the best selfless service, the best in reflective thought, the best in the creative arts, and the best in human wisdom. The humanities offer the best chance of demonstrating . . . the sweetness of cooperation over the sour destructiveness of the adversary mind, the painful glory of creative effort over the dull boredom of the low aim.

In academia, you can listen to an American scholar statesman, Vartan Gregorian. His life story illustrates how the humanities can play an ever broadening public leadership role not only in universities but also in libraries, foundations, and the public arena. Rising from a childhood in the Middle East, he has been an exuberant humanist with a rich sense of humor. To his early experience as a member of the Christian minority in a benevolent Muslim community, he has added insights learned from American Westerns and the practical wisdom of people on the streets of Tabriz, Beirut, and Paris, through Texas and California, Philadelphia and Providence, to New York. And, he is supporting excellence in the humanities to bolster democracy in post Communist Russia as well as postmodern America. Dr. Gregorian personifies even as he supports the American tradition to add new immigrants and new ideas without subtracting or discarding the old.

The United States is the only world civilization whose institutions were created entirely in the age of print. Democracy and humanism alike emerged from the culture of the book.

We now need—more than ever before—the skills of humane judgment that the humanities help develop—guiding us back from information on the Internet to the knowledge embedded in books—and moving on to the kind of practical wisdom that has historically made America both stable and innovative. Reaffirming the liberal arts core of our educational system and the capacity it fosters for humane dialogue will help equip us better to understand at a deeper level other nations as well as our own. A dangerous but increasingly interdependent world needs a deepening dialogue of cultures if we are to avoid an enduring clash of civilizations.

James Billington
Librarian of Congress

Preface

"All memorable events transpire in morning time
and in a morning atmosphere
Morning is when I am awake and there is a dawn in me.

"We must learn to reawaken and keep our selves awake,
not by mechanical aids, but by an infinite expectation of the dawn."
Henry David Thoreau

WHEN SELECTING THE ART to appear on the cover of this book, our publisher, Martin Scrivener, observed that he liked the painting selected but wondered why we had chosen a picture of a sunset. In a nutshell, his question about the painting on the cover is the primary question of this book. Are we approaching sunset or sunrise? In the face of the dramatic changes around us—from globalization, new technologies, global terrorism, natural disasters, or social, cultural, and intellectual change—is America facing sunset or dawn?

The thesis of this book is that we face dawn. The book is an unabashed celebration of America and its promise. Our argument is that the core idea of the Declaration of Independence, grounded in the fundamental right of each person to the "pursuit of happiness," is an inexhaustible mainspring of change and an anchor for hope. We aim to connect emerging global change with the pursuit of happiness and to show that change today is not only consistent with this principle but also, in fact, caused by it. We believe that a major shift is just beginning: a tectonic shift in human consciousness and life that will unfold from the dynamics of the pursuit of happiness. Far from portending cataclysmic ends, such as "the death of God," the "death of humanity," the end of language, or the degradation of ethics, politics, values, and art into barbarity and banality, the enormous shift under way is a shift toward renewal and dramatic creative growth in all areas of spiritual understanding, economics, value, and life. We are not yet able to comprehend the final shape of this creative renewal. As a result, we tend to be more aware of what is ending, and this can create a feeling of fear and foreboding.

We realize that many fear the changes under way and do not share our sense of optimism and hope. We are also aware that there is a darker side of globalization: that many do not yet participate in its benefits and that it links in a global network those who are disaffected. This is a moral issue to be taken seriously, but we do not believe that it constitutes a counternarrative or alternative to the pursuit of happiness. Because of these concerns and anxieties, we also attempt to uncover the roots of contemporary fears about the future and critics of America's culture and society. We find that these efforts to create a critical counternarrative to the pursuit of happiness are based in ideas from either Romanticism or early modern rationalism. Often, the philosophical roots of these ideas are not consciously considered or examined. When brought to attention, it becomes clear that neither of these systems of thought is applicable in today's world. It is time to reclaim the civic space that is too often held hostage by fear and by "civic vandals."

A new renaissance is possible if we choose to let go of these counternarratives, take responsibility for civility and civic space, and align the many forces of change around a renewed, broadened, and intellectually charged affirmation of life and the pursuit of happiness. This is a project for a new generation of young leaders, to whom this book is primarily addressed. There is a great hunger for such a culture, as the proliferation of gurus, psychologists, radical religions, and "lifestyle consultants" makes clear. Cultural leaders in America need to reclaim the territory being lost to such figures and to "philosophies" that are all too often shallow and unreflective. As the Scripture reminds us, "Where there is no vision, the people perish."

Go back and read, even aloud, the Declaration of Independence again. It distills a powerful, crystalline vision for our world, and its message resounds as loudly today as it did in the halls of Philadelphia some 230 years ago. This book concerns the deeper meaning and importance of those framers' intentions. It is about their pivotal phrase, "the pursuit of happiness," which reminds us that the moral sentiments of a people matter.

For those of you who want a digested version that is intended to spur you on to action, we would take no offense if you turned to the back pages and considered, then acted on, our *Thirty-Six Propositions*. Nail them to your civic wall or the city hall door, if you like. (Where the propositions appear in the text, they are set in **boldface**, although their wording may differ slightly from that at the end of the book.)

This book is written in the hopes that it will spark a national dialogue about civil society, rooted in the humanities, and that it will ultimately inspire a new generation of humanistic leaders. Our argument evokes a version of the natural law, but its values and perspectives are thoroughly contemporary.

This book is not an anti-American diatribe or a volley in the fruitless "culture wars" that have produced more heat than light. We aim for a reasoned and thoughtful analysis that is open to serious thinkers—of all persuasions and points of view—who are interested in constructive work. The only rule is that logic and reason, rather than expressions of taste and shrill emotion, guide dialogue. We aim to provide an argument: *for* something. The book makes practical suggestions, brings up the subject of money, and has a deep appreciation for what we call *spiritual capital* and the ultimate humanism of commerce. This book is a resounding call for everyone in civic, governmental, and commercial life to renew our culture.

The question raised by our publisher and by this book is, of course, classic. At the end of the Constitutional Convention, Benjamin Franklin, that archetypical American, observed that during the course of the debates over the formation of the new American government, he had mused on the sun carved on the back of the chair in which George Washington sat to preside over the convention. He said that he had wondered many times through the ups and downs of the debate whether the sun were a rising or a setting sun. In the end, he announced, it was a rising sun.

It still rises!

Acknowledgments

CREATIONS, LIKE THE WRITING OF A BOOK, are the result of generosity and support from many sources. Although we as authors are responsible for the specific line of argument, along with any errors, oversights, or omissions, our lives, thoughts, and work on this project have been fed by many family members, mentors, and supporters. First, we wish to acknowledge the understanding, support, and thoughtful ideas from members of our families. Here and there, our mutual gratitude will occasionally branch into individual acknowledgments.

On the Massey side of the ledger, these personal thanks include my sons, Alec and Cameron, who give me the rewards and challenge of fatherhood with daily lessons in love, humility, and joy. I am proud and blessed to be their father.

On the Malloch side of the equation, appreciation goes first to Beth. I (Ted) am truly blessed to have a supportive and loving wife, three sons, and a daughter, who as a true family, undergird and encourage whatever I have chosen to do in this life. Ian, Trevor, and Nigel are like the horses often pulling the sled ahead and have been a source of near constant satisfaction, pride, and meaning in my existence. "Princess" Morgan is just that, a godsend whose charm and grace make possible even the dark and heavy hours. Thank you all.

Together, we are deeply grateful to the Ford Foundation, which provided principal support for a national summit that we created at the Aspen Institute to launch the dialogue furthered by this book. The Foundation also supported our participation in an international conference in Florence, Italy, on the future of the humanities, as well as time for us to complete the draft of this work during a hot, cloudless Tuscan July in 2004. We are also grateful to the John Templeton Foundation for major support of this work, specifically, for funding for a television documentary to explore the ideas outlined in this book. Support for other elements of this project came from the National Endowment for the Humanities, the Kettering Foundation, Deborah Simon, and Lilly Endowment. To all of these, we are deeply grateful.

Our thinking has been enriched by so many. It has become a cliché to thank one's parents, but it would be impossible for me (Scott) to have had the drive or intellectual discipline for a project like this without the tremendous love, dedicated faith, and intellectual brilliance of my parents, S. H. Massey, Jr., and Dorothy Tinsley Massey. They formed the bedrock of my life and personal faith. My sister, Jane, is also an inspiration and essential part of my life and thoughts. Ted notes that it is a biological truism that without one's parents, one literally would not have entered the world. But my (Ted's) parents have been so much more. Ted and Dorothy lived for their sons, they educated and raised us in faith, but most important, they lived by example—an example of faith, hope, and charity that makes America what Lincoln called "the last great hope of humanity."

Great teachers and mentors also contributed to this work. It is impossible to list them all. Among those we can name here are (for Scott) James Billington, John Compton, Maxine Greene, John Lachs, George Steiner, Nelson Andrews, Peter Jennings, Eva Meredith, Kenneth Swanson, and Leonard Bernstein. For Ted, Ella Rhodes and John Greech enriched my early life; William Harper, Malcolm Reid, Dave Frantz, Grady Spires, and Thomas Howard, in college; and Christian Bay, Paul Marshall, and foremost, the brilliant Bernard Zylstra, in graduate school. In professional life, academe, politics, nonprofit service, finance, research, diplomacy, and strategy—wherever our careers have led us—we have both tried to listen, dialogue, and learn perpetually—from many leaders, friends, and fine minds.

Whenever a book with dual authorship appears, one wonders who wrote this or that and whether the whole exercise turned into a series of compromises driven to a lowest common denominator. In this case, we have had the distinct pleasure to work together over many years as intellectual equals and profound friends and to develop a deep sympathy and respect for each other's ideas. Our friendship started years ago at the Aspen Institute and continues in a number of common projects and with the Indiana Leadership Summit. This book grew out of our common belief that America deserves a deep cultural renewal and that a sound argument can be made for the outlines of that renewal. We hope that the argument here will be our contribution as public intellectuals and participants in civic culture to that renewal. Each of us has his distinctive academic backgrounds and specialties as well as broad interests that together made this large undertaking and the scope of the argument possible. This could not have happened without sustained conversation and friendship, which, after all, is the essence of the humanities.

We appreciate the Indiana Humanities Council for its support for our work in applying some of these ideas in projects in Indiana. Special thanks as well to Lorenzo, our Tuscan villa landlord, who wrestled with the Italian postal service to retrieve a shipment of books and a laptop for our work on this book.

We are grateful especially to our brilliant and supportive publisher Martin Scrivener, whose faith in this work has been an inspiration. We are also extremely grateful to Nicholas Capaldi, editor for this series, who was a positive contributor and colleague in reframing several chapters and in the final preparation of the manuscript. We are indebted to both gentlemen for their generosity and companionship in the work.

1

The Pursuit of Happiness

THE PURSUIT OF HAPPINESS is not as simple as it sounds. To take hold of this idea is like pulling on a thread that unravels the whole cloth. As a result, the argument of this book covers a wide range of topics that may seem unrelated at first—topics such as globalization, the origins of the liberal arts, smart technologies, entrepreneurship, art, and even the connection between economics and the human spirit. Connecting these usually disconnected topics is intentional, even unavoidable when thinking about happiness in today's world. Indeed, these diverse issues must be reconnected through the twin concepts of "the pursuit of happiness" and "spiritual capital," along with a new sense of the "transcendent," if we are to develop the wisdom and culture to guide the forces of innovation and globalization that are transforming our world.

The rapid changes affecting America and the world have been led by economic and technological forces. The cultural dimensions of this change have been largely ignored in the process. Without a significant advance and innovation in the realm of culture and value, the great economic and technological gains of the recent past are exposed to great risk. A new, life-affirming humanities framework that reconnects economics, culture, science, art, and leadership with the life of the spirit is critically needed to mitigate this risk. More important, it is needed to create a just and flourishing human society.

Because we have been accustomed to separating these issues into separate spheres of fact and value, economics and culture, science and faith for so long, rebuilding a coherent synthesis will take time and effort from many thinkers. Certainly, a single book like this one can only begin the process in the hope that gaps and juxtapositions of ideas stimulate further work. At the same time, we believe that the models of happiness, spiritual capital, and social-economic justice developed here are deeply consistent with one another and therefore provide a unifying central core around which the many other issues can be understood and reconceived. Also central is a renewed reference to transcendence, to concepts, values, and realities that lie outside our systems of thought and action but that give shape and impetus to thought and action.

Specifically, this book raises and answers three questions.

1. What are the core values of America?

2. Why do they have to be renewed?

3. How do we engage in the process of renewal in today's global knowledge economy and society?

The pursuit of happiness is a uniquely American dynamic and outlook that continues to shape our destiny and now affects people around the world. The core values of American culture are enunciated in the Declaration of Independence: specifically, in the idea of the "pursuit of happiness." The Declaration establishes strong connections among economic liberty, religious liberty, and political liberty. This has important implications for spiritual, political, and human capital. A reaffirmation of that connection enables us to seize the full potential of the tremendous changes and innovations under way in the world, as well as to overcome the seductions of relativism, victimization, and nihilism. Moreover, the Declaration calls for both

expansive vision and prudence, connected virtues that are needed to address the great challenges and opportunities of the twenty-first century.

These core values require renewal because of the challenges
of globalization engendered by modern commerce and technology. The renewal requires recapturing and reenergizing the common vision of the pursuit of happiness shared by the major sectors and institutions of economics, politics, and nonprofits.
Liberal education under the leadership of the *humanities* must
play a crucial role in providing this shared vision. Three distinct
but related themes to explore are (1) the tremendously expanded
scope of innovation and the vast canvas on which future leaders
will be able to create; (2) the need for relationships and dynamics
among institutions (especially private corporations, government,
and nonprofits) to be rethought on a scale to match expanding
opportunities; and (3) the need for institutions of higher education in general and the humanities in particular to rise to the challenge and play a leading role along with business and government in articulating these new relationships and cultural trans-
formations. Further, we raise the question, Will a new generation
of leaders seize the opportunity to shape these forces of transformational change into a more humane world guided by the pursuit of happiness?

Why are education in general and the humanities in particular so crucial here? As Michael Oakeshott put it, human beings
are distinctive in that we are free to choose how to interpret experience.[1] The human predicament is characterized by the opportunity and ordeal of having to choose and to create ourselves continually and our understanding of the world within the limits set
by experience and the world. This task is accomplished through
learning and intellectual creation. Our imagination and intelligence are the faculties used in defining ourselves as individuals
and in giving meaning to experience; this engagement is called
learning and is the source of our humanity.

Increasingly, learning is the source of economic prosperity.
Liberal learning is the unique ordering of our experience in reason

and imagination; it is what makes us unique individuals. One of the most important ways in which we learn to utilize our intellect and imagination is in reconstructing the thoughts of another person. Through this process, we subsequently learn to find our own voice and the ability to add value to new information and activity. It is only through interaction with our cultural inheritance that we become who we are. Our cultural inheritance is a set of achievements and practices, not a doctrine to be learned by rote. The content of this inheritance is conveyed in the form of meanings. The inheritance is recreated for each new generation through learning. This conception of humanity and liberal learning has important implications for structuring all institutions, especially today in the context of a global knowledge economy and society. Today, across all sectors, the key assets are knowledge and the ability to add new value and increased meaning to information.

As important as they are, the physical sciences and the social sciences cannot play the role of developing interpretative perception and value, because they are not equipped to explicate norms. The explication of norms is a distinctively humanistic enterprise. In the recent past, the humanities have failed to live up to that role. To begin with, the rapid expansion of higher education in the 1960s failed to convey the *ethos* of liberal learning. Moreover, treating literature as data to be explained by hidden structures rather than as an expression of inherent value, reductive views of humanity, treating human beings as if they were merely complicated animals or clever machines, the view that people are nothing but the product of their environments, victimization, and the hostility to spirituality and religion—in short, the social-scientization of the humanities—have often created an adversarial relationship between the academy and the larger culture and its traditions. Specifically, the failure to understand economics, which led to hostility toward modern commerce and its larger social connection, has frayed the common bond that previously sustained commerce, politics, and nonprofits, such as higher education, in a commonwealth of thought and action.

The necessary process of renewal will involve four steps. First, we explicate the fundamental norms of the Declaration of Independence and basic values and experiences furthered by the humanities. Second, we identify current challenges and opportunities presented by the huge shifts in knowledge and globalization. Third, we propose a restructured civic structure and dynamics for business, government, and nonprofits. Fourth, along the way, we outline strategies and policies that are consonant with the first three steps.

As a concluding coda and to facilitate action, we offer *Thirty-Six Propositions* at the end of the book as a framework for a rising generation of young leaders to use as they create what will amount to a dramatically new world. These propositions come from the chapters in this book. The propositions are highlighted in boldface in the body of the text and are presented together as a framework at the end of the book.

Core Value: The Pursuit of Happiness

We hold these truths to be self-evident, that all men are created equal, that they are endowed by their Creator with certain unalienable rights, that among these are Life, Liberty, and the pursuit of Happiness.

With this frank, bold statement, the American founders created the genetic code of American life and experience. Affirmed as self-evident, this deceptively simple statement contains the seeds for what may be most distinctly American about our culture, our government, and our expectations. This passage contains a revolutionary idea that is still unfinished: an idea that continues to unfold and to reveal new insights, new experiences, and new opportunities to leverage advances in science, technology, economics, the arts, ethics, and politics for expanding human happiness. Here is the key to an outlook that has shaped our destiny and that today is rapidly expanding to shape the destinies of people around the world.

This transcendent right is not derived from any government, institution, or individual and is unalienable. What is this revolutionary idea? Simply this: that all human beings have the fundamental right to live freely and to pursue happiness. Notably, these rights precede the Bill of Rights and are said to come from the "Creator." This means that they are transcendent rights—rights not derived from any government, institution, or individual—and, as the document states further, "unalienable"; that is, they cannot be transferred by any contract or agreement that anyone might make freely or under duress. These rights form a core, or nucleus, of what it means to be human. Life, liberty, and the pursuit of happiness are affirmed to be basic and equal. The right to live, the right to liberty, and perhaps most remarkably, the right to pursue happiness are presented as coequal, fundamental, and transcendently grounded rights of all human beings. **It follows that the central purpose of government, culture, and work is to put power in the service of human flourishing.**

To our ears centuries later, the phrase "pursuit of happiness" is so familiar that we simply pass over it without much thought. When we do pause to reflect, the phrase may seem less clear; it may even raise questions. For example, where does the emphasis fall: on *pursuit* or on *happiness*? And what, after all, is happiness? To pursue is not necessarily to attain, and so it may seem that Jefferson and Franklin were proposing a fundamental right to something unattainable, something forever on the horizon. The pursuit of happiness may suggest Robert Louis Stevenson's conclusion to *El Dorado*: "to travel hopefully is better than to arrive."

How do we understand "the pursuit of happiness": as an endless pursuit without substance or as an intrinsic, substantive activity? Can a convincing case still be made for this idea of the pursuit of happiness as ethically sound and politically wise? To live as a human being, beyond the basic biological fact, is to pursue the full exercise of one's abilities within a range of opportunities and risks. Liberty defines the range of risk and opportunity necessary for action; happiness provides the range and direction of pursuit; and life is the outcome of active pursuit and opportunity. From this perspective, to prioritize security over risk is to diminish the opportunity to live.

Precedents for this understanding of what it means to be human and to live a fully human life can be found in Greek and Roman classics, a body of thought with which the founders were deeply familiar. Aristotle's concept of *eudaimonia* perhaps comes closest to the conception. Most frequently translated as "happiness," *eudaimonia* is a compound term made up of the Greek "*eu*," meaning "good" or "beautiful" or "well formed," and the word "*daimonia*," which is derived from the noun "*daimon*," which means a demigod, or spirit. Thus, *eudaimonia* means to be good spirited, to have a beautiful disposition, to have a well-formed character, or inner life. These descriptions should be understood as three descriptions of the same thing, descriptions that map different features of the same psychic terrain.

Because the term is derived from the concept of a demigod, furthermore, it carries overtones of a god dwelling within us, inspiring us with good spirits, beauty, and a well-ordered soul, or disposition. Socrates, when transported in thought, characteristically said that he was listening to his personal *daimon*. In the *Symposium*, Alcibiades compares Socrates to a popular trinket sold in the markets of the time—a rather ugly clay figure that could be opened to reveal a beautiful golden figure—a *daimon*—within.

These ideas and images from Greek philosophy and religion are important clues for how we can understand happiness in a new way today, a way closer to that in the Declaration. Over time, our concept of happiness has become somewhat threadbare and thin. It needs renewing, and the Greek originals are a good source for renewal.

Put simply, the concept of *eudaimonia* provides a much richer and more complex model of happiness than we typically use today. *Eudaimonia* is based in character; it entails a series of concrete actions and dispositions, as well as a transcendent source of these characteristic dispositions and actions, that is, a source that lies outside (transcends) action and that gives action shape and meaning. Like the center of a circle which generates the circle but is not one of the points making up the circle, happiness, in this view, originates from a point outside its constitutive activity and arch. To use another analogy, a gymnast imagines a center of gravity around which to create disequilibrium and motion through space; in a similar way, *eudaimonia* hinges on a center of gravity outside its own motion and action.

Here is a conception of happiness as an inner disposition and activity linked with a transcendent source, not an external goal or accoutrement. Understood in this vein, *eudaimonia,* or happiness, is activation of the profound core of a person, not a superficial trait, such as a sunny disposition or good luck. Happiness is, thus, more like a scientific description designating a specific structure of character and pattern of activity. Like a fine work of art, the many capacities and drives of a "happy" person are well fitted and integrated into a complete, finished whole; they are not disjointed and at odds. Integrity is the descriptive hallmark of happiness as a basic pursuit. A happy character is permeated with aesthetic qualities: it is beautiful and graceful. Further, in addition to integrity, which describes *eudaimonia* as a static pattern or psychic architecture, *eudaimonia* is essentially dynamic. *Eudaimonia,* or happiness, is activation and engagement of all the appetites, desires, and capacities that make up a person in a balanced, well-adapted way. When optimally engaged, these capacities take the shape of an integrated pattern, a whole, individual person. The actions of such a happy person are also beautiful and graceful because such a person does the right thing at the right time for the right reason and in the right way. The behavior is appropriate, suitable, and well intended. It has many of the qualities of a work of art.

These are some of the Greek intellectual precedents that inspire the ideas of life, liberty, and the pursuit of happiness in the Declaration. The existence of these precedents, however, does not diminish the revolutionary use of these ideas by Jefferson and Franklin. With the Declaration, we see these ideas applied as the founding principles of a new limited government and society. **The founders' bold wager that the purpose of society is supporting each individual's definitive right to live freely and to pursue happiness as a critical choice is the most daring political experiment in history.**

The Critics

For many critics of American culture, now and in the past, "pursuit" may seem to be just the right term. To critics, American culture fails to establish a sufficiently serious social ideal and order. The source of this criticism comes from romanticism. As Sir Isaiah Berlin explains in *The Roots of Romanticism*:[2] "[Romanticism] introduces for the first time . . . a crucial note in the history of human thought, namely that ideals, ends, objectives are not to be discovered by intuition, by scientific means, by reading sacred texts, by listening to experts or to authoritative persons; that ideals are not to be discovered at all, they are to be invented" (p. 87). He notes further that "those are the fundamental bases of romanticism: will, the fact that there is no structure to things, that you can mould things as you will—they come into being only as a result of your molding activity—and therefore opposition to any view which tried to represent reality as having some kind of form which could be studied, written down, learnt, communicated to others, and in other respects treated in a scientific manner" (p. 127).

As these passages suggest, and as Berlin goes on to argue, romanticism is the intellectual source of political and cultural opposition to forces that are supposed to be external or reality based. The allowance of market forces and the external, independent exercise of choice is a failure of imagination and creativity on the part of political, economic, and cultural leaders, from this perspective. Because of such assumptions, social critics of America tend to fault American culture for a lack of social engineering and the creation of an overarching ideal, or vision.

Interestingly, as Berlin and others have noted, this set of assumptions provided the basis for fascism and Nazism, on the right, and for socialism and communism, on the left. As a result, both the political left and the political right in today's world share a common intellectual ancestry in romanticism. The application of romantic assumptions about the primacy of will to actual political institutions and societies produced some of the more horrific examples of human suffering in history. Combined, the exterminations justified by right-wing romantic political philosophies and left-wing theories have produced massive human suffering and loss.

Today, ironically, the vestiges of this set of assumptions survive mostly in the political rhetoric and critique of the far left. The major sources of discontent with American society still come from a romantic aesthetic that finds satisfaction in social ideals managed through central power acting to bend society toward that ideal. Again, as Berlin writes, "there is even such a thing as romantic economics . . . where the purpose of economics, the purpose of money and trade, is the spiritual self-perfection of man, and does not obey the so-called unbreakable laws of economics. . . . Romantic economics is the precise opposite of [laissez-faire economics]. All economic institutions must be bent toward some kind of ideal of living together in a spiritually progressive manner" (p. 126).

Still building on this idea from romanticism, the media, most academics, and many in cultural leadership roles seek a "spiritually progressive" social ideal. During a recent presidential election, one of the network anchors began his response to a convention acceptance speech by observing that he "did not hear any sweeping or bold vision outlined in the speech tonight." The dominant theme of discontent centers on this search for a social ideal, and when one is not found, on intense scorn and distaste for the effects of its absence. The current editorial pages of the *New York Times* are a continuing set of variations on these themes of romantic longing and scorn. This assumption also explains why the private sector and free markets are viewed in these circles as morally corrupt, as sources of commercialism, materialism, and individualism. Because the power of a central government is needed to bend society toward an ideal, those on the romantic left favor increasing the power of government over the private sector and see the distribution of economic resources through the agency of government as the way to uplift money and trade to "the spiritual self-perfection of man," to use Berlin's phrase.

It is interesting to note that this social structure, with a governmental elite bending society toward a social ideal that is invented and authenticated by its self-evidence among the elite, mirrors the Cartesian model of thinking, in which valid ideas are not generated in give-and-take social dialogue or through the actions of history but come through the mind's conception and the idea's self-evidence. (We will have more to say about the structure of Descartes' ideas and their impact later in the book.) This structure can be found replicated over and over in both intellectual and practical settings in modern culture. It constitutes the repeatable pattern of the "wallpaper" of modernity.

Unfortunately, political debate today does not go deeply enough to uncover these intellectual assumptions and to test them. Testing them, either from a conceptual standpoint or in terms of their historical impact, reveals serious shortcomings. Lacking conscious intellectual assent or deep critical analysis, however, these ideas have shrunk to become a matter of political taste, like a taste for a certain type of music or food; when not satisfied, the response is disgust and repulsion, the typical response when taste is offended. Hence, an intellectual engagement of these assumptions has been replaced by increasingly shrill commentary and expressions of disgust and loathing. If, as the right has largely concluded, the assumptions of romanticism about the primacy of will and social ideals are an untrustworthy basis for policy, the left too would do well to seek another foundation. The same general critique can be applied to the right whenever views on the right express simply a political taste for the primacy of individual will and private interest over a social "herd" instead of clearly stated ideas grounded in reality and open to testing and debate.

In addition to these critics, even friends and general observers too often comment that American culture appears to be caught up in an endless, perhaps pointless, pursuit of happiness. From the absurdities of pet rocks and fads in music, consumer goods, and entertainment, critics often see the mass popular culture and life of America as mindless and purposeless pursuit. From this point of view, the free expression of human economic appetites that produces the madcap range of American life is both unattractive and morally suspect.

To read the phrase "pursuit of happiness" in this way, however, misses both a core meaning of the term *pursuit* and an alternative vision of the meaning and value of American culture and economics. In its core sense, a *pursuit* means a vocation, or calling, not a running after some elusive, unattainable goal. This meaning is still current when we speak of someone's career as a pursuit or perhaps identify a favorite activity, such as golf, as a pursuit. On this reading, a pursuit is not something extrinsic but something intrinsic to a person's core being and character. In this sense, pursuits uniquely define a person because they identify the characteristic activities that make one an individual. This dynamic model of individuals finds the essence of a person in activity, not repose; in choice, not will.

The idea of the pursuit of happiness also raises many questions for us today. Over time, the term *happiness* has come to carry overtones primarily of chance, good luck, and prosperity, as a check in a current dictionary will show. The first connotation of happiness today, therefore, is a state of mind that results from good luck. Because luck and prosperity are external and largely outside our control, happiness, understood in this way, is not a deep structure of choice or personal virtue. In light of this prevalent meaning, the term *happiness* strikes our ears as superficial. One layer below this set of meanings is a connotation of pleasure, which with its hedonistic overtones is likewise regarded as superficial, perhaps morally suspect.

In addition to these top two layers of meaning, however, there are deeper and older meanings that connect to personal character. The deeper and older meanings refer to the satisfaction and gratification a person receives from being well adapted, well suited, and well fitted. Being well adapted and well fitted conveys a quality of appropriateness and, therefore, a sense of both aesthetic and moral worth. The idea of a well-adapted or well-fitted character also implies a certain understanding of an individual as a set of capacities and aptitudes that require shaping and integration to form a whole person. In this sense, happiness begins to convey something of deep personal meaning and value. But ironically, for contemporary ears, a "happy turn of phrase" (i.e., a well-fitted phrase) conveys a deeper sense of happiness than does the phrase "a happy person" (someone who experiences good luck, prosperity, or pleasure).

Understanding *pursuit* as the choice and effort required by a personal vocation or cherished activity and *happiness* as a well-fitted character begins to suggest why the *pursuit of happiness* could be seen as a transcendent and basic human right. Understood in this way, the *pursuit of happiness* does not imply that happiness is an external thing to be sought but instead an inner calling, an intrinsic dynamism, integrity, or optimal integration and full engagement of a person's powers and faculties. All the terms used here are critical for unpacking this idea—optimal, integration, engagement, dynamic, and powers. From this perspective, the pursuit of happiness is the effort to create a well-articulated set of personal capacities into a vocation. The goal is individuality, the lived achievement of the abilities, talents, and interests that most distinctively define each person. The idea also implies an internal scale of values, a kind of self-governance, since developing an individual's unique set of abilities also requires an effort to connect and balance the different inclinations into a well-integrated whole.

Like a well-crafted chair or cabinet, a well-fitted character requires that the pieces and parts of a person be well designed and hang together. This description emphasizes static qualities of the pursuit of happiness: their architectural plans, if you will. The idea also needs to be understood dynamically.

Viewed from this perspective, the pursuit of happiness is an optimal (not maximal) degree of activity that engages the whole person. The result of such optimal activity is integrity, that is, happiness, or a fully integrated, optimally active individual who knows his or her own mind, abilities, and excellences and who therefore is capable and worthy of self-rule, or liberty.

From this concept of happiness, we find ourselves back at the idea of liberty. This suggests that the three rights—life, liberty, and the pursuit of happiness—are interlinked and need to be understood in terms of one another. Like pier mirrors in eighteenth-century ballrooms, these three concepts reflect one another and are contained in one another. Liberty, thus, is not simply freedom from authoritarian government or tyranny or other external constraints. Instead, liberty is the capacity that a happy person possesses for self-rule and self-government. Thus, although liberty may be necessary for happiness, it is also true that happiness is necessary for liberty. Again, critics of American culture often search in vain for some source of social concern or constraint in American culture to temper individualism. It is clear from experience that Americans are highly engaged in civic and community service and activity. Yet to many critics, the source of this duty is a mystery.

The mystery is resolved in happiness. Out of the integrity of character that defines happiness comes the authority and capacity for self-governance and for individual life and action in community with others. In this view, justice is expressing one's distinctively individual "pursuits" while not interfering with the self-expressive practices and pursuits of others. The interactions among self-governing individuals is homeostatic, to use the term from systems theory. That is, the interactions between individuals and the community become a self-regulating mechanism, like a thermostat. The source of this self-regulation cannot be understood, however, apart from the concept of the pursuit of happiness. Compare this with Plato's definition of justice in the *Republic*, 433b: "*Kai men hoti ge to ta autou prattein kai me polypragmonein dikaiosyne esti*" (translation: "Thus, justice is the practice of the self without interfering in the practices of others"). Here, Plato defines justice as self-practicing (*autou prattein*—that is, the practice of the distinctive abilities of the self—in such a way that one does not interfere (*polypragmonein*—literally, *polypractice*) with the self-practicing of others. Plato argues that a just society is homeostatic and self-regulating, because allowing each and every person in the society to practice a personal ensemble of interests and abilities would at the same time constitute an ecological system, that is, noninterference with others. In more colloquial terms, we could say that Platonic justice is being oneself and not interfering with the efforts of others to be themselves.

A New Universal Paradigm

Although many other cultures and societies have placed a high value on life, and many have placed a high value on liberty, this American emphasis on the pursuit of happiness seems distinctive, even unprecedented. Throughout most of history and for perhaps most cultures, the pursuit of happiness is considered secondary to other goals and even possibly unattainable. From the perspective of history and culture, the pursuit of happiness hardly merits a position as one of three definitive and transcendent human rights. Justice, salvation, property, equality, duty, service to the state—are not these more important than happiness? What government, besides the American, was self-consciously established to put the full force of its power and policy behind the pursuit of happiness of its citizens?

To a remarkable degree, American politics, economics, and culture have evolved to embrace the pursuit of happiness as a central drive and value. Here, the founders made a bold wager that a real (i.e., nonutopian) society and limited government can be created with the purpose of supporting each individual's definitive right to live freely and happily. This experiment is one of the most monumental risks in history.

From this experiment spring a set of exhilarating attitudes about the future, the value of risk, the intrinsic justice and spiritual expressiveness of economic activity, the role of law and gov-

ernment as positive forces, popular culture, innovation, the value
of ordinary life, and justice. With the pursuit of happiness as the
true north and magnetic pole of this experiment, American society raised anchor from the past to set its sights on the future. In
charting a course into the future, America redefined and chan-
neled the energies of economics, government, law, cultural
expression, and ingenuity toward continuous improvements for
life. To a remarkable degree, American society and culture are
defined by their dedication to improve the prospects of human
happiness.

Even more than life and liberty, the pursuit of happiness
defines the quality of American life and drives America's "soft
power." People around the world are attracted to the pursuit of
happiness that permeates and energizes American movies,
music, clothes, popular foods and entertainment, and active
lifestyles, as well as large-scale organizations of economic and
political power. The universality of this appeal is expressed brilliantly by the Nobel Prize–winning novelist V. S. Naipaul in his
October 1990 Wriston Lecture:

> The universal civilization has been a long time in the making. It
> wasn't always universal; it wasn't always as attractive as it is
> today. The expansion of Europe gave it for at least three cen-
> turies a racial taint, which still causes pain. In Trinidad, I grew
> up in the last days of that kind of racialism. And that, perhaps,
> has given me a greater appreciation of the immense changes
> that have taken place since the end of the war, the extraordinary
> attempt of this civilization to accommodate the rest of the
> world, and all the currents of that world's thought. . . . A later
> realization—I suppose I have sensed it most of my life, but I
> have understood it philosophically only during the preparation
> of this talk—has been the beauty of the idea of the pursuit of
> happiness. Familiar words, easy to take for granted; easy to
> misconstrue. This idea of the pursuit of happiness is at the heart
> of the attractiveness of the civilization to so many outside it or
> on its periphery. I find it marvelous to contemplate to what an
> extent, after two centuries, and after the terrible history of the
> earlier part of this century, the idea has come to a kind of
> fruition. It is an elastic idea; it fits all men. It implies a certain
> kind of society, a certain kind of awakened spirit. I don't imag-

ine my father's parents would have been able to understand the idea. So much is contained in it: the idea of the individual, responsibility, choice, the life of the intellect, the idea of vocation and perfectibility and achievement. It is an immense human idea. It cannot be reduced to a fixed system. It cannot generate fanaticism. But it is known to exist; and because of that, other more rigid systems in the end blow away.[3]

We would do well to pay attention to Naipaul's insight. We would do well to stop and take note of the astonishing role played by the pursuit of happiness as a defining ideal of American society and increasingly of global society. The idea is now so engrained in everyday life that we can easily fail to appreciate the radical nature of the outlook or the pervasiveness of its impact. We also fail to appreciate the underlying, powerfully humane impulse behind the idea. To elevate the day-to-day happiness of each person to the central purpose of government and culture and to work to put power in the service of human flourishing is a revolutionary form of humanism.

The Challenges

In the face of the serious ethical issues facing the world—hunger, poverty, genetic engineering, racism, disparities in wealth, war, and religious conflict—is the pursuit of happiness a trivial moral framework for the future? Given the staggering political challenges that lie ahead in managing social commitments, such as Social Security, environmental challenges, and international law and policy in the light of globalization, can the pursuit of happiness provide substantive guidance?

What are the prospects for the American experiment today? In the face of the tremendous changes and threats in the world, what, in fact, are the prospects for human happiness and flourishing? Do new technologies increase or diminish the prospects? Does globalization, with its attendant shifts of jobs and wealth and juxtaposition of cultures, offer a support for happiness, or does it undercut the possibility? What does the explosion of new knowledge offer? Is the emerging picture of the universe and life compatible with a concept of human flourishing and happiness, or do the sciences reveal a hostile and pointless existence? How are religious conflicts and beliefs to be understood? Is the world-wide growth of religious communities a positive development or the approach of a new dark age of irrationality and fanaticism? Can science, religion, the arts, and the humanities move beyond the culture wars to forge a new, positive synthesis?

Is the humanism of the founding period outdated or even harmful in today's world? Postmodern humanists argue that rea-son is always a mask for power and that love is a mask for dom-inance. The twin humanistic values of the Enlightenment and the romantic period are thus on notice as false foundations. What is to replace them? Is a new humanism possible today that can embrace the everyday happiness of individual people, religious faith, science, economics, and politics in an enlightened, life-affirming culture, like past humanistic cultures? Or will the drive of a popular culture—already flexible enough to embrace virtu-ally every variety of expression and experience—simply overtake culture, leaving humanists on the sideline as marginalized crit-ics? Is this desirable?

Without deeper intellectual and creative energies, will the sources of personal values and innovation begin to dry up? As technology increases the impact of human choice and amplifies the significance of individual choices and character, how can these human abilities be cultivated without an enlightened humanism? Is a worldview from the humanities still important for business, government, and nonprofit leaders? In today's world, innovation and creativity are also more critical than ever. How are these deeply human capacities to be sustained and stim-ulated outside the framework of creation in the arts and human-ities? To feed the sources of creativity and personal meaning, how can the public humanities be rethought and reinvented as a positive, life-affirming, and sophisticated culture?

The rapid, interlinked dynamics of smart technologies, the growth of knowledge, and globalization have created a perfect storm of change. In many ways, the social, political, and intellec-tual forces unleashed by the American experiment have created this perfect storm. Can they continue to carry us through? What new paradigms and discoveries are available today to provide a new framework for an intellectually sound and defensible humanistic, civic culture organized around the pursuit of happiness? In light of the dramatic changes around the world today, what are the practical prospects for human happiness in the future, and what strategies are most likely to promote it? What needs to be rethought to be successful? What needs to be preserved? Perhaps most important, how do we as a new generation stand in the shoes of the founders to look out at the world as bravely as they did and ask how to innovate and create so that every human being in the world has the opportunity to enjoy the God-given, unalienable rights of life, liberty, and the pursuit of happiness?

The adventure begins here.

Notes

1. Michael Oakeshott, *Rationalism in Politics and Other Essays* (New York: Liberty Press, 1991).
2. Isaiah Berlin, *The Roots of Romanticism* (Princeton, NJ: Princeton University Press, 1965).
3. V. S. Naipaul, "Our Universal Civilization" (New York: Manhattan Institute for Policy Research, 1990 Wriston Lecture).

2

Economic Humanism as Spiritual Capital

T HE SPIRITUAL VALUE OF MONEY, commerce, and prosperity is a subject of conflicting views in today's world. New technologies and globalization are driving commerce and markets to new levels, and rising standards of living are spreading around the globe, but the core issue of the spiritual value of this activity remains largely unresolved. The issue especially troubles the conscience of religious and humanities leaders. Building on ancient cultural perspectives rooted in agrarian and nomadic societies, many religious and humanities leaders still see money and commerce as tainted with immorality and greed. From the viewpoint of traditional culture, the spiritual and the commercial are polar opposites.

In *Les Misérables*, Victor Hugo captured one dimension of the concern about economic activity that tends to polarize views of economics, namely, the differences between the production and the distribution of wealth. He wrote:

All the problems which the socialists propounded . . . may be reduced to two principal problems.

First problem:

To produce wealth.

Second problem:

To distribute it. . . .

England solves the first problem of these two problems. She creates wealth wonderfully: she distributes it badly. . . . Communism and agrarian law think they have solved the second problem. They are mistaken. Their distribution kills production. Equal partition abolishes emulation. And consequently labor. It is a distribution made by the butcher, who kills what he divides. It is therefore impossible to stop at these professed solutions. To kill wealth is not to distribute it.

The two problems must be solved together to be well solved.[1]

A further source of uneasiness comes from a view that the generation of wealth in the private sector is somehow debased at its core. As Sir Isaiah Berlin noted in the comment quoted earlier, according to the cultural view that grew out of romanticism, "the purpose of economics, the purpose of money and trade, is the spiritual self-perfection of man."[2] That is, money and trade, although valueless in themselves, gain value as a result of being directed toward a higher social ideal. From the perspective of romanticism, the everyday world of facts and commerce is a realm of illusion that pales in comparison with the ideals of the imagination. Oscar Wilde expresses this general outlook succinctly in these lines from *A Picture of Dorian Grey*: "actual life was chaos, but there was something terribly logical in the imagination. . . . In the common world of fact the wicked were not punished, nor the good rewarded. Success was given to the strong, failure thrust upon the weak."[3]

This general view of the tension and contrast between the spiritual and the commercial continues to be a dominant point of view on the political left and among many religious and humanities leaders. But are these categories still appropriate for a global knowledge-based economy? Is economics, when driven by knowledge, still a zero-sum game, as it was in agrarian and industrial times, or can the pie continuously expand due to the continuous expansion of knowledge and technology? **We believe that the old, traditional gulf between the spiritual and the eco-**

**nomic can be bridged because there is a spiritual basis for eco-
nomic activity, a "spiritual form of capital" that is linked to
human and social capital.**

The social science literature is replete with empirical and theoretical treatments of the role of entrepreneurship in economic
development. The concepts of social capital and human capital
are by now rich and extend beyond economics to management,
human resources, political science, and sociology. Indeed, both
have become in recent decades important: twin pillars in capitalism and democracy at the individual, corporate, societal, and
global levels.

Less developed by far is the emerging concept of spiritual
capital and its attendant impact on entrepreneurial behavior. The
concept is pregnant with possibilities drawing on the intersection
of economics and religion in such classic works as R. H. Tawney's
Religion and the Rise of Capitalism and Max Weber's *The Protestant
Ethic and the Spirit of Capitalism,* as well as more recent thinking
on economics and development. But does "spiritual capital" pass
the so-what test? Is it possibly the hidden motivation in economic booms as far apart as Ireland and Singapore? How exactly does
religion affect economic behavior at both the macro and micro
levels? Is it a secret ingredient in the very nature of entrepreneurship? Can we fully demonstrate the relevance, validity, and
potential of the notion that spiritual mores and underpinnings
demonstrably affect economies and firms?

The hypothesis is that, in the ultimate sense, spiritual capital
is the missing leg in the stool of economic development and
entrepreneurial activity, which includes its better-known relatives: social and human capital. *Entrepreneurship,* derived from
the French, originally meant the acts of persons who managed a
company and assumed the risks of business. The verb came from
the same as *to undertake;* it therefore suggested proactive behavior. At the outset of the nineteenth century, French economist J. B.
Say used the word for those who shifted economic resources out
of an area of lower and into an area of higher productivity and
greater yield. But that action was shaped by the culture and

delivered in trust. Trust was at the base of business activity, and it was ultimately formed and informed by religious and spiritual beliefs and traditions.

Social Capital

The term *social capital* first appeared in print in 1916 in the context of academic debates on the decline of America's cities and close-knit neighborhoods. In present decades, sociologists have given the term more credentials. Glenn Loury used the phrase in 1977 to describe sources of certain kinds of income disparities, and Pierre Bourdieu described it as one of the forms of capital that help account for individual achievement. Chicago sociologist James Coleman has also employed this concept throughout his opus of contributions.

So far, most of this literature has little to say about how managers or entrepreneurs can actually increase an organization's stock of social capital. And most recently, Nan Lin's trilogy on social capital—theory of social structures and action, theory and research, and foundations of social capital—has further refined what has become a more and more widely used social construct now in popular parlance.

The World Bank defines social capital as "the norms and social relations embedded in social structures that enable people to coordinate action to achieve desired goals."[4] Robert Putnam, the Harvard political scientist, describes it similarly. "Social capital," Putnam writes, "refers to features of social organizations such as networks, norms, and social trust that facilitate coordination and cooperation for mutual benefit."[5]

In the realm of politics, Robert Putnam's landmark 1993 book, *Making Democracy Work,* convincingly demonstrated that the political, institutional, and economic value of social capital is substantial. In 2000, Putnam brought out *Bowling Alone,* a scholarly and provocative account of America's declining social capital. Numerous findings of comparative economic studies by the World Bank and the United Nations corroborate Putnam's thinking, namely, that some regions of the globe lag behind while others thrive due to their social capital.

In their book *In Good Company*, Don Cohen and Laurence Prusak examine the role that social capital—a company's "stock" of human connections, such as trust, personal networks, and a sense of community—plays in thriving organizations. Social capital, it turns out, is so integral to business life that without it, corporate action—and consequently productive work—is not possible. Social capital involves the social elements that contribute to knowledge sharing, innovation, and high productivity. In their recent seminal study, Cohen and Prusak point out that social capital consists of the "stock of active connections among people, the trust, mutual understanding, and shared values and behaviors that bind members of human networks and communities and make cooperative action possible."[6] Social capital makes any organization or any cooperative group more than a collection of individuals intent on achieving their own private purposes.

It seems apparent that in the same sense, some firms thrive as a result of their stored social capital, whereas others fail for its lack. But what is the origin of such stocks within a firm? Mission statements and goals carried on laminated cards or placed in hallways do not produce values per se. In entrepreneurial firms, founders' values often carry exceptional weight for numerous generations to propel companies to extraordinary results. In past decades and centuries, many of these values grew out of religious impulses or were grounded in the spirituality of their founders. ServiceMaster, Herman-Miller, and Mail Boxes Etc. are more recent examples of this same phenomenon.

Human Capital

The term *human capital* first appeared in "Investment in Human Capital," a 1961 *American Economic Review* article by Nobel Prize–winning economist Theodore W. Shultz. Economists have since loaded on much baggage to the concept, but most agree that human capital comprises skills, experience, and knowledge. Some, such as Gary Becker, add to the mix personality, appearance, reputation, and credentials. Still others, such as management guru Richard Crawford, equate human capital with its owners, suggesting that human capital consists of "skilled and educated people."

Newer conceptions of total human capital view the value as an investment. Thomas O. Davenport, in *Human Capital: What It Is and Why People Invest It*, looks at how a worker performs, depending on ability and behavior. For him, the choice of tasks also requires a time-allocation definition. The combination of ability, behavior, effort, and time investment produces performance, the result of personal investment whereby a multiplicative relationship enhances the outcome. Davenport further elaborates a notion of worker investment, describing what it means to work in the relationship nexus between the employee and the employer. He explains in mostly anecdotal, company-specific detail how companies that treat workers as investors can attract, develop, and retain people. These people both derive great value from their organization—and give so much in return—that they create a competitive advantage for their firms.

A further quantitative refinement in this field is the so-called business case for return on investment in human resources. Such works as *The HR Scorecard*, by Jack Phillips, put forward a measurement case for viewing the employee as a human asset. It has become almost trite to recite the fact that in both economic development and firm behavior, the most important assets are the human ones. In firms that grew out of a spiritual formation, there is typically a great commitment to so-called people development, as workers are viewed as stewards and co-owners who deserve and need continual nurturing.

Spiritual Capital

A Web search does not yield much on the topic of "spiritual capital." An index search in Amazon.com yields much the same result. A search turns up such items as *Seven Capital Sins* by Bishop Fulton Sheen, *Witchcraft and Welfare in Puerto Rico,* and an out-of-stock pamphlet on capital cities and urban planning. So why bother? Is this a virgin field or a foolish endeavor? Can the development literature fill in any of the gaps and provide an adequate framework for spiritual capital? Is the study of entrepreneurship a potential hotbed of spiritual capital?

In the past two decades, more recent debates in development macroeconomics have revolved around debt management and relief, the appropriate role of the price mechanism, trade policy, the effect of policies in developed countries on the rest of the world, and the transition from closed, or centrally planned, economies to open-market ones. At the micro level, questions concerning choice of planning techniques have continued with a renewed debate on whether capital-intensive projects and globalization produce the most growth. At the United Nations in particular, there has been an emphasis on human economic development in a broadly defined sense. Few studies to date have asked how entrepreneurship is originated or sustained. The religious basis of entrepreneurship is anecdotal at best. Some comparative studies have argued that entrepreneurship surfaces in many centers around the world, most notably in places like Bangalore, India, as a result of Hinduism; Chile, where evangelical sects have proliferated; and, of course, offshore Chinese communities.

But development is not simply a goal of rational actions in the economic, political, and social spheres. It is also, and very deeply, the focus of redemptive hopes and expectations. In an important sense, as Peter Berger reminded us in *Pyramids of Sacrifice*, "development is a 'religious category.'"[7] Even for those living on the most precarious margins of existence, development is more than a matter of improved material conditions, although that is included. Development is clearly a vision of redemptive transformation. This sense of spiritual capital is founded on an understanding that all resources are entrusted to people for good management and development. This form of capital underwrites the disposition of both individuals and groups to preserve and develop a wealth of resources for which they are accountable here and later. Thus, spiritual capital is about the entrusting of responsibility and a care for the creations such responsibility exhibits. Within various religious traditions, creative obedience or norms in economic activities are one primary way for adherents to acknowledge and demonstrate faith.

Within this frame of reference, economic development, often led by the entrepreneurial acts of risk taking, can be seen as a process through which persons and communities learn to care for and use the resources that sustain life. **Economic development can be viewed as creative management of endowed resources by stewards who act on their faith commitments.** Here, genuine economic growth is guided by normative laws, character, and principled habits and practices that take into account the preservation needs of human beings, their environments, and their physical, mental, social, cultural, and spiritual lives. In the ultimate sense, spiritual capital may be the third, or missing, leg in the stool that includes its better-known relatives, namely, human and social capital.

International relations theory and development economics since the 1980s have similarly argued that in a globalized economy, as more advanced western and northern nations progress in technology, capital formation, growth, and diversification of economic sectors, a "feedback" effect on culture, politics, and society occurs. Has this model omitted a formative cultural impact on economics that sets the cycle of progress in motion? If economics affects culture, does culture affect economics? To what extent are spiritual variables, or spiritual capital, the missing component ignored in much of recent academic inquiry and policy analyses of global economic growth? To what extent does the entrepreneurial activity that commences and fuels such growth depend on spiritual variables?

One can rightly ask which factors and issues economists and practitioners should add to their future studies to gauge this missing link. In other words, can we operationalize spiritual capital so that the concept and empirical findings can be made more plausible and evident in economic activity? Because the notion of spiritual capital is closely connected to ongoing debates on trust, corruption, governance, sustainability, and entrepreneurship, this is a critical next step. Some things to look at include

- the role and scope of personal religious ethics on private economic decisions, which face all persons and groups;

- the exegetical, economic, and historical roots and traditions that give rise to contrasting work ethics and economic systems;

- the role of societal institutions based on faith, ranging from companies to trade unions to political parties to non-governmental and intermediating structures;

- interpretations and practices concerning interest, investment, inflation, growth, government authority, charity, and trade in various spiritual worldviews;

- the impact of religion on conduct and rules as employees and employers, consumers and producers, and citizens at every level of existence;

- the degree to which religious practices and policies directly or indirectly affect economic behavior, choices, and economic policy;

- the role of spiritual capital as the basis for entrepreneurship.

There may be no one set of religious principles regulating any given economic polity, but all religious peoples, regardless of their faith community, make individual and collective choices in which personal faith, colored by longstanding and deeply rooted historical religious traditions, are highly relevant and important factors. Given the importance of entrepreneurs in the economy, it can be argued that their spirituality is given amplified expression in the business activity they commence and sustain over time.

Spiritual capital can become a useful concept for a vital feature of economic development that has been largely overlooked in modern theories of development. Indeed, the often-used terms *social capital* and *human capital* themselves are based to a large extent on the existence of good faith, trust, stewardship, a sense of purpose, and other moral characteristics that cannot persist in the absence of the piety, solidarity, and hope that come from religion and spiritual sentiments. When this is lost, societies and economies often decline rather than grow. When this abounds, societies, economies, and companies prosper.

Models of Spiritual Capital

In light of these thoughts, here is a model for spiritual capital. To be economical, this model will be compressed into basic elements that advance an understanding of human and social capital and add depth and dimension to the pursuit of happiness.

Spiritual capital is a form of capital that aligns with its cousins, both human capital and social capital. In that sense, spiritual capital provides an overarching conceptual model and structure that gives definition to human and social capital. In other words, spiritual capital is a unifying theory for the commonly used models of human and social capital. But it is also more. It is a normative, directional dimension that gives meaning and purpose to all human activity.

Spiritual capital has real and measurable economic value, especially in connection with entrepreneurship and the creation of not only innovative products and services but also prosperity. As an overarching theory for human and social capital, spiritual capital helps to complete the picture, to demonstrate the conceptual linkages and relations of human and social capital, and to tie these forms of capital to core economic processes of the creation of prosperity, one of the core issues of economics. In spiritual capital, wealth creation and generation are paramount.

There are three possible models for the origins of prosperity. (1) The sources of prosperity are *mysterious*, as in mythology, guarded by gnomes and spirits under the earth and reluctantly given to humans, who must use magic and trickery to gain access to these sources of wealth. (2) Prosperity grows through tribal, corporate, and national conquests that seize wealth from others. (3) There is an understandable human capacity that is the creative source of prosperity. The first two views assume that wealth is a preexisting, fixed resource that simply moves from one column to another. The third view posits that prosperity is open and expandable and that it can be created by both human knowledge and effort. Spiritual capital represents a theory of this third way.

In other words, the concept of spiritual capital posits that the sources of prosperity are knowable, can be spread by knowledge and education/training, and are human capacities that can transform the world. This, of course, does not mean that spiritual capital is human to the point of ultimately excluding a transcendent point of reference, or cocreator. That is, spiritual capital as conceived is deeply rooted in natural law/theology and the reality of God's action in the world. At the same time, the concept has sufficient structure and integrity to define a set of human and social capacities that can operate independently of any theology or specific set of religious beliefs. Again, theology—and likely some theologies more than others—may provide the deepest conceptual base for spiritual capital, but the theory can be articulated on its own terms. For now, we will simply point to these issues without deeper examination. Perhaps the **overriding moral question of these times is how we unleash each person's distinctive capacity and personhood to create prosperity**.

The importance of the concept and its effect increases dramatically in the context of the emerging knowledge and innovation economy. In the past, attention has focused on financial capital and physical capital as static, limited assets to be accumulated, invested, traded, and managed. The source of economic prosperity was taken for granted, largely, as an existing condition to be exploited. In this context, economics was modeled more on the basis of resource management in large systems, with growth and development coming largely from the management of costs. Today, it is impossible to "cost cut" to prosperity, innovation is unleashing a new wave of economic disruption to major industrial systems, and new interest is being focused on the very origins of prosperity. This feature of economic activity has often been left shrouded in mystery or simply taken for granted, but spiritual capital can help to shed light on it. In its simplest form, spiritual capital can be defined as the grounding and integrative system of human and social capital.

Spiritual Capital as a Dynamic Model

Spiritual capital is not simply the set that includes human and social capital. Nor is it simply a static quantity or asset, like money in the bank. Instead, spiritual capital is a dynamic and complex cultural system that helps to create both human and social capital. The general dynamic model for spiritual capital is shown in Figure 1.

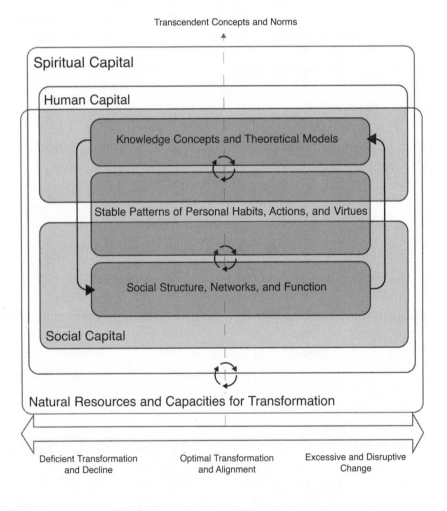

Figure 1 Model of Spiritual Capital

As this model illustrates, spiritual capital is a system of three interlocking systems, or virtuous cycles, which in turn are linked through a virtuous cycle with the natural world and its resources, systems, and physical capacities. Starting at the top, we see human capital as emerging from the virtuous cycle feedback loop that connects a person's knowledge (including formal education, technical knowledge and skills, normative stories and narratives, conceptual models, metaphors, paradigms, and core beliefs, or worldview) with a person's stable patterns of action, habit, and virtue (i.e., excellent performance). Social capital can be said to consist of the virtuous cycle feedback loops between stable patterns of individual behavior and larger social structures, networks, functions, and activity.

The model also maps a spectrum of value for spiritual capital by means of the bipolar line at the bottom of the model. The dotted line through the systems to this line projects an optimal alignment of the systems and their virtuous cycles and an optimal level of transformation for each level, that is, an optimal alignment and transformation of natural resources, social organization, individual behavior, personal knowledge, and hence spiritual capital. Aristotle might call this optimal alignment and transformation of nature and spirit the "Golden Mean." The right end of the line points toward excessive disruptive change that destroys alignment and transformation, and the left end of the line points toward a deficiency of transformation, or a deteriorating status quo. This dimension of the model suggests that some forms of spiritual, human, and social capital may be more optimal than other models for producing alignment and transformation that create value, which in economic terms equates with greater prosperity. This model also suggests that optimally, prosperity is aligned with increasing value, measured in noneconomic categories—personal knowledge, human behavior, and social structure and activity—as well as increasing value in the natural world.

In passing, it might also be noted that this model implies that the interaction of human beings and culture with the natural world is transformative and adds value to nature. In fact, it suggests that nature is incomplete without the transforming effects of humanity. Instead of seeing the impact of human interactions with nature as destructive or debasing to nature, this model suggests that, optimally, human interactions with nature add value to the natural order. Of course, some human interactions with nature can also be destructive. Knowing what and when to build and what and when to keep is as old in wisdom literature as Genesis itself. But this view provides an alternative to the view that nature unaffected by humanity is *the ideal*. Instead of setting nature and humanity at odds or loggerheads, the model acknowledges the fact that human beings are part of nature and suggests that a point of integration of human and natural transformation can exist that adds value for both human beings and nature. The garden may be one good metaphor for this integrative zone of mutual good.

The dotted line that breaks through the system and points toward concepts and norms that lie outside the system also underscores points made in the prior chapter about happiness and character. In other words, this model of spiritual capital is consistent with the understanding of happiness and character described earlier. In the previous chapter, we noted that *eudaimonia,* or happiness, entails a series of concrete actions and dispositions, as well as a transcendent source, that is, a source that lies outside (transcends) action and that gives action shape and meaning. The model of spiritual capital as outlined in this section is deeply consistent with this reading of happiness and character. Indeed, the isomorphism of the model helps to show the deep linkages among the core concepts of the pursuit of happiness, personal integrity or character, spiritual capital, and the sources of economic prosperity.

Here is a conception of happiness as an inner disposition and activity linked with a transcendent source, not an external goal or accoutrement. Here also is a model of spiritual, human, and social capital that links the structures of these systems with a transcendent source as the Archimedean point from which a plumb line of alignment and transformation is found. As Gödel's *Incompleteness Theorem* showed, a contained system cannot be complete; other truths exist outside, or transcend, any closed system of truths.

Levels of Organization and Autonomy

Behavior and social organization can be separated from theory and can be borrowed and exported like capital. This is illustrated in the spiritual capital model, which implies that the various levels linked by the feedback loops each have a degree of autonomous existence. A person's habits and skills, for example, are not completely determined or linked to that person's knowledge and beliefs. The behavior has a degree of autonomy from personal knowledge, and personal knowledge has a degree of autonomy from behavior.

Put differently, a person's knowledge and beliefs underdetermine the person's actions, habits, and virtues. We do not always act in accordance with our knowledge or beliefs, and sometimes we perform better than we know. From our family or community, we may have learned habits that are grounded in a set of ideas we do not explicitly know or believe or hold dear any longer, but the behaviors grounded in those ideas may be transmitted with a degree of independence from their originating concepts. Similarly, we may be taught a set of ideas that we can explicitly state but not transform into behavior. It is possible to know the Apostle's Creed without translating that knowledge into habits and actions. Or we may have learned explicit knowledge and have worked to apply that in stable patterns of personal behavior and virtue.

Likewise, social structure and activity are underdetermined by the behavior of the individuals who make up the society. This helps to explain how a society can continue to function according to the general rule of law and with a functional level of trust in spite of the fact that individuals in the society may be dishonest or may break the law. A tipping point may be reached, of course, when too many individuals violate the basic rules of law and trust, but a strong social system can continue to exist despite violations by members.

This helps to explain how some societies may develop social structures and activities without individuals in that society adopting the core ideas that originated the social structures. Many of the functional features of a market economy, for example, may be put in place in societies that lack economic theories consistent with markets. Because social structures can develop a level of integrity and robustness of their own, these systems may function relatively well, at some degree of separation from a core theory to explain them. From this perspective, social capital may be borrowed or imported from another society that has created the knowledge that generated a specific social structure, such as markets.

In this case, the importing society's social function is dependent on the originating society to underwrite the long-term functioning of the system through its knowledge investment. In this way, relatively large and complex social structures and functions can emerge and operate with a minority community that understands the essential knowledge or theory that creates the system, a fact that is more often lamented than celebrated. It may be celebrated, however, as an example of the tremendous efficiency and effectiveness of knowledge as a cause of widespread effects. The knowledge of a very few can be leveraged exponentially to affect global populations.

In other words, theories matter, ideas matter, and knowledge matters. But there is no simple causal path by which core knowledge and theoretical models directly affect human action and social action. It is enough that optimally, or largely, consistent structures and functions can be created to put the core ideas into practice. Because of underdeterminination, patterns of action very rarely model their core theories to a maximal degree. Even in the best of circumstances, the best to hope for is approximation. When theory and practice come very close to coincidence, we may experience a rare moment of almost perfect virtue, but this proximity is as difficult as it is rare. We have many stories about this concurrence, but they are often fables. It is good to long for a community in which all personal and social behavior is transparent, and every person has a complete grasp of the ideas that radiate through this transparency, but ours is not that world.

Spiritual Capital as Code: Freedom and Self-Organization

Our overall definition and model of spiritual capital describes spiritual capital as a set of linked systems. Spiritual capital also needs to be understood as a type of code, such as the genetic code, the grammar of a language, or the code for a computer program. From this perspective, spiritual capital is more narrowly defined in terms of embedded concepts and theories. That is, spiritual capital is embedded and transmitted principally at the level of knowledge. Spiritual capital is what can be dubbed cybernetic.

A code is an underlying pattern that determines how a system will operate and change in relation to other systems and the environment over time. Some codes are closed and are used to replicate identical structures and functions every time. Other codes are open and self-organizing. Using matrix code levels to preserve a core invariance through change, open codes interact with the environment and may themselves change and develop over time without collapsing or completely changing themselves at any one time. For example, the grammar of a language is hierarchical in this way, and this allows a language to change its grammar drastically over time without ever ceasing to be grammatical at any one time. The genetic code also uses a core alphabet and structure to create many various forms of life; through those organisms, the genetic code continues to develop at the level of individual organisms and species.

Spiritual capital is like grammar or the genetic code in that it is open, self-organizing, and develops new forms over time through its operation in individuals and at the level of society.

This self-organizing capacity, combined with the level distinctions among knowledge, personal behavior, and social structure/function, introduces a significant range of freedom into the system. Core knowledge may be applied experimentally in many ways in personal behavior and in society. The distinction of levels, the underdetermination of levels, and the relative autonomy of the structures at each level help to explain the notion of human freedom that is implied by spiritual capital and the subsets of human and social capital. Without these levels and ranges of freedom, there would be no reason to teach spiritual capital; it would simply be the operating code of human beings and their societies.

Understood from this perspective, it is also clear that spiritual capital inheres most concretely in a distinctive set of concepts and core knowledge that can be explicitly stated. The creation of these core concepts, the continuing interpretation and critique of knowledge they generate at all levels, and the careful transmission of core ideas, beliefs, and knowledge are essential activities in the creation, application, and transmission of spiritual capital as well as human and social capital.

In essence, the principal function of spiritual capital is intellectual and spiritual. Spiritual capital, as the genetic code for human and social capital, is built primarily though learning, the generation of knowledge, and the intellectual and spiritual practices that promote creative response and receptivity to novelty from outside any formal system of knowledge. Some truths exist outside any consistent set of propositional truths. The growth of spiritual capital requires both intellectual capacities—the capacity to build and test propositional systems and formal models—and the capacity to be receptive to truths from outside the system as well as to new paradigms.

This also means that religious, scientific, academic, corporate, and educational institutions, together with the emerging new smart technologies and the vast pervasive computer archives and data, are the primary contexts in which spiritual capital develops. That said, there are also important roles for government and private enterprise to play in relation to spiritual capital and its systems of knowledge. Today, new "translation platforms" need to be created that define social theories and models that engage spiritual capital formation in effective ways to the work of government, the social sector, and business. Defining these platforms and defining core concepts integral to optimal spiritual capital formation is an area ripe for serious scholarly research and development. It would seem to serve as the foundation for broadening the base for prosperity and for expanding the pursuit of happiness.

Market Forces

What are market forces? Simply put, they are the forces of supply and demand in an unregulated market between buyers and sellers. Together, these forces determine the price at which a product or service is sold and the quantity that will be traded. This continual interaction of supply with demand in turn shapes a market economy. Markets influence and are influenced by the moral character of culture. Adam Smith was the first to argue that markets, through the discipline of continuous dealings, instill virtues, such as honesty. Prudence ties moral concepts to practical result.

Over time, more and more intellectuals, including the likes of Charles Dickens and Max Weber, have argued that markets erode virtue. Post-Kantian philosophers have divorced moral virtue from practical consequences by adopting the fact/value dichotomy. This has made markets and perceived moral virtues antagonistic to each other. The present-day culture wars rage against bourgeois values. The alleged distinction between the pursuit of happiness and private property has been at the heart of the left-wing critical historiography of the American experiment for more than a hundred years.

Can we restore the moral acceptability of commerce? Put simply, do markets matter in a way that enhances the pursuit of happiness? The answer is yes. Private property is essential to a market economy; a successful market economy makes possible human flourishing, or the pursuit of happiness as we have explained it. Tibor Machan has argued that the value of commerce as a means for enriching our lives and enhancing culture can be appreciated apart from showing that it contains moral worth in and of itself as a form of human activity.[8] The prevailing position that commerce is immoral needs to be reconsidered in light of human nature and *eudaimonia*. If the central drive is to achieve flourishing lives, and if our lives consist of creative, productive connectedness to the world that surrounds us, commerce (as a pursuit of prosperity), because it facilitates that connectedness with the world, should occupy a more elevated role in our lives than is acknowledged by many worldviews and far too many humanists.

As Douglas North argued in *The Rise of the Western World*, the affluence we now know and expect is a rather new and unique phenomenon.[9] It is only several centuries old, and it commenced in western Europe. The abject poverty and recurring famines of the past have been largely overcome in the West. Relative abundance is a rare historical achievement made possible by efficient economic organization. The key to this growth entails institutional arrangements and property rights that create significant incentives to channel individual effort that brings the private rate of return close to the social rate of return. The factors that bring about economic growth are innovation, economies of scale, education, and capital accumulation. But what actually causes growth to occur? Simply put, an economy and its participants must be convinced that incentives are in place to undertake socially desirable activities.

Even MIT's noted popular economist, Lester Thurow, agrees that, "since the outset of the industrial revolution, when success came to be defined as rising material living standards, no economic system other than capitalism has been made to work anywhere. No one knows how to run a successful economy on any other principles. The market, and the market alone, rules."[10] The forces of market capitalism expand on individuality and self-interest to produce rising standards of living for all. These market forces cater to wants and desires of consumers like no other system before. Capitalism itself, it turns out, is successful because it is continually evolving and adapting to new and emerging situations and environments. Market capitalism harnesses the inexhaustible energy of human appetites to fuel virtuous cycles of development and prosperity. These self-reinforcing systems sustain the vast edifice of a highly diversified society, including its highest activities and achievements.

The great alternative experiment, endorsed by and supported by so many prominent humanists—the attempt to create a context for human flourishing without markets, namely, Marxism—has been an abject failure. With the fall of the Soviet Union and of communism in all but a few places, the scandalous history of Marxism and Leninism has been exposed. The cost in lost productivity and in human lives was unprecedented in all of human history. For about a hundred years before, the ideas of Karl Marx were viewed as bankrupt in most philosophic circles, but the weight of his *Das Kapital* was shored up by the barrel of a gun and/or nuclear missiles, thereby prolonging its hideous effect on the totalitarian societies and cults of personality that had been created. Socialism found its basis in an economic theory that did not work.

The humanities have had an uneasy relationship with capitalism, markets, and industry and at times have been capitalism's sharpest critic. The humanities would like to be free of labor and household economics—free to think. Sometimes, they have sought justification for market ills, market failures, or past injustices. Today, like it or not, the humanities are both part of a larger market for goods and ideas and a wellspring of sentiment for the liberty and freedom that only markets allow.

The humanities need to support free and democratic institutions and thereby build both civic culture and individual purpose. In that sense, the humanities would be a bulwark of the system that allows them the independence they seek and the respect they deserve. In return, is it too much to ask that the humanities in a nonpartisan fashion defend the system that makes them possible, that pays for their very existence? Without some form of wealth creation, there would be no arts or literature, no film or drama, or any organization to support philosophy or religion. Capitalism is the most prosperous and productive system of economic behavior ever invented, and for the foreseeable future, it is the fuel of the globally integrated system. There is no third way, no democratic socialism. There is a unified global capital market, even if, as Frans Tropenaars argues, there are as many as seven cultures of capitalism, ranging from Japan to Germany, and over-powered often by the United States' version, due to its political, economic, military, and media might.

An uneasy alliance with the market is the de facto relation between cultural and academic institutions, but this is clearly of limited value. In the new global economy, the market is also making possible numerous new opportunities for the public and for culture. Some of these involve different kinds of joint ventures or partnerships with corporate and other partners, while others create new competitors—new publishers, media companies, history channels, and the like—founded to take up the mainstream civic space abandoned by others.

It is time to try on the Emperor's new clothes: to take responsibility to understand today's economic principles with a view toward contributing value to the process. As Tom Friedman and many other writers note, a new synthesis of economic growth, ethics, environmentalism, politics, and culture is necessary to address the challenges before us. A developed theory of spiritual capital can help to provide a conceptual bridge among these interests and provide insight as to how the sectors can work together in new ways to globalize prosperity and the pursuit of happiness.

Notes

1. C. E. Wilbour, trans., *Everyman's Library* (New York: Alfred A. Knopf, 1997), pp. 829–830.
2. I. Berlin, *The Roots of Romanticism* (Princeton, NJ: Princeton University Press, 1965), p. 236.
3. O. Wilde, *A Picture of Dorian Gray* (Edina, MN: Abdo Publishing, 2002), p. 227.

4. World Bank, *World Development Report* (Washington, DC: World Bank, 1985), p. 29.
5. Robert Putnam, ed., *Democracies in Flux: The Evolution of Social Capital in Contemporary Society* (New York: Touchstone, 2001), p. 7.
6. D. Cohen and L. Prusak, *In Good Company: How Social Capital Makes Organizations Work* (Cambridge, MA: Harvard Business Press, 2001), p. 14.
7. Peter Berger, *The Sacred Canopy: Elements of a Sociological Theory of Religion* (New York: Anchor, 1990), p. 96.
8. Tibor Machan, *Capitalism and Individualism* (Christchurch, NZ: Cybereditions, 2002).
9. Douglas North, *The Rise of the Western World: A New Economic History* (Cambridge: Cambridge University Press, 1976).
10. Lester Thurow, *The Future of Capitalism* (New York: Penguin, 1997), p. 18.

3

The New Century and Its Challenges

THE RAPID, INTERLINKED DYNAMICS of technology, the growth of knowledge, and globalization have created a perfect storm of change—all unleashed by the American experiment. The next few decades appear to hold much that is likely to prove both chaotic and revolutionary. The old, industrialized world and its attendant national organizations seem to be coming to a screeching halt. Gerald Ross wrote brilliantly about this collective phenomenon in his book *Toppling the Pyramid*, noting that we are entering an altogether different era in human and commercial history.[1] Because populations and markets around the world are gearing to technologically advanced products from the developed world, international trade is likely to continue its phenomenal growth in the coming decades. What are the prospects of the pursuit of happiness in the context of such change? How does a renewal of our culture and a new model of civil society relate to this change?

Globalization

What does the future hold for the organizations, private and public, that make up the emerging social order? How must concepts of security and cooperation shift to adjust to a new era of global interaction and connectivity? Like it or not, we are all starting this trek to the pinnacle of an uncertain future, full of both new opportunities and high risks, given the degree to which the economy is increasingly linked and interdependent.[2]

Revolutionary processes are shaping the future of the global organization over the next decade which will alter both the human condition and enterprises: everywhere and forever. These dynamics include the globalization and digitalization of industry, a radically new geopolitical world situation of seeming disorder, the struggle for ecological balance, the death and rebirth of ideologies and ethnicity, and the brewing conflict over indigenous culture. Increasingly, religious belief and the worldwide growth of religious affiliation are a force to be reckoned with, as both a force of resistance to change and a potential dynamic support for transformative change. If they understand these new dynamics of change and their challenges, organizations and institutions will be more likely to prosper from the coming integrated global economy and to contribute to the creation of new social orders. If they fail to act or simply react too late, institutions will suffer the consequences and cease to exist, withering into meaninglessness or chronic decline.

The challenges that frame the contours of the future are shaping the "state of the world." No organization or institution— large or small; state, national, or multinational; commercial or nonprofit—can escape the emerging organizational operating system that will shape our common destiny. **Trade in ideas and products and the movement of people are leading the way to a more global and integrated yet complex technological civilization. The world's operating system is in effect being rewritten today.**

Over the past decade, the financial world became part of what has often been dubbed the "global village," as capital markets were tied and integrated in all the major financial centers: the United States, Europe, and Japan. Manufacturing and service industries are following the very same pattern of development.

The graph in Figure 2 explains the underlying forces that have made globalization a reality.

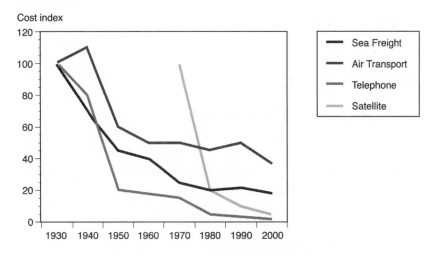

Figure 2 The Forces Behind Globalization
(Center for Regional Economic Development, Case Western
Reserve University)

As this graph shows, there has been a steady trend over several decades for costs related to location to decrease dramatically. As these costs have dropped, so too has the economic value of location, and the marginal costs of work at a distance have become less and less significant. With collapsing costs for transportation, telephone, and satellite communications, it is possible to distribute operations around the globe. This cost collapse has driven the globalization of industries and continues to make the logic of globalization all but inevitable.

Now in addition to these cost dynamics, smart production technologies allow companies to manufacture as close as possible to their markets in any part of the world. This "global localization" features such breakthroughs as just-in-time manufacturing, computer-integrated manufacturing, real-time global capital flows, mass customization, and workplace automation and robotization. The dynamics of the integrated digital global economy are forever changing the way business is conducted and the way we organize our work and our societies. Technology is the key. Being digital is central to this connected economy. The number of Internet users today is over 1 billion and by 2006 should be closer to 2 billion.[3] The Internet is increasingly at the core of connectedness. Kevin Kelly of *Wired* magazine paints a vivid picture of this future scenario in his book *Out of Control*,[4] and this scenario is rapidly coming to fruition, even if some persons, places, and organizations are lagging far behind.

As we move through this global economic transition, a new Schumpeterian cycle of "creative destruction" and intense entrepreneurial competition and repositioning is sweeping through like a tornado. Nonmaterial investments, such as R&D, education, and training, are becoming far more important than material investments. Likewise, the knowledge infrastructure has become more urgent than the physical infrastructure. The secret to the profit-maximizing behavior of global entrepreneurs reveals that R&D drives long-run productivity. The integrated global digital economy opens up a world of opportunity rather than one of designed constraints. The global impact of the Web and e-business has been compared to the invention of printing, the voyages of discovery, or even the Renaissance. Increasingly global organizations are cognizant that their most valuable asset—intellectual property—is rooted in their intellectual and human capital. So, competition for human talent and innovation, wherever it is located, is very much a part of an integrated global future.

Just as the value chain has been disintermediated, so too has the traditional organizational model. The tightly structured command-and-control hierarchy characteristic of most of the twentieth century is giving way to the fast-moving, entrepreneurial, adaptive, and agile model of the twenty-first century. The new organization is no longer a single entity with hard organizational boundaries and walls but rather an extended, permeable network consisting of an increasingly streamlined global core, market-focused business units, and shared support services. This model of a permeable organization with geographically dispersed networks of expertise and precisely targeted data-driven services is relevant for the nonprofit, educational, and public sectors, as well as for the private business sector. This organizational model lends itself to the flexible teaming, select alliances, and increased outsourcing characteristic of competition. This networked, nonlinear, coherent organization is neither centralized nor decentralized. Its dynamism, flexibility, and openness form the foundation of what some have dubbed the ultimate organization.

Much has been made of the end of the bipolar world—the historic close of the cold war and the dissipation of the Soviet Union. Our entire civilization and the processes of socialization and identification are being rethought.[5] Can changes so dramatic help but change the ways we are organized? Is this not a ripe time for the humanities to again supply thoughtful answers to perennial questions?

Risks are most likely to appear on the fringes of the triad. As Southern Hemisphere regions attempt to gain their foothold in the globalizing economy, the flash points will increasingly appear where Northern Hemisphere encounters Southern Hemisphere, where "connected" societies touch "disconnected" societies, and where scientifically advanced cultures encounter traditional and religiously grounded cultures. The modernization of Islamic countries across a long belt stretching from Morocco in North Africa to Indonesia and the southern island of the Philippines is proving to be the line of demarcation and the hotbed of radicalization and its offspring: terror. Dealing with this clash of civilizations is, as Harvard's Samuel Huntington[6] and the Pentagon's Thomas Barnett[7] have described it, the inflection point for the coming decades. It is not limited to this line of tension, however. Even within advanced Western cultures, religious fundamentalism on the right and radical environmentalism, antiglobalization, and labor leaders opposed to trade agreements that make labor susceptible to global competition form a loose federation of common interests that could coalesce into an internal inflection point.

In this emerging integrated global digital economy, national prowess will be calculated by five distinct factors: (1) global economic competitiveness, (2) media power, (3) position inside global networks, (4) military strength, and (5) soft power. With this last factor, cultural and human capital is represented by social and personal skills with powers for innovation, rapid change, high ethical standards to facilitate flexible teaming and social action, and public infrastructure that supports entrepreneurship, continuous learning, transparency, and fair rules of play. Power has a special definition in the disorder of this emerging new world. The new relationship, which has emerged in the UN Security Council and at the World Trade Organization, is profoundly multipolar and multinational. The United States as a hegemonic power will likely lead such alliances and be the main thrust of economic development as the world's strongest and largest economy.

Globalization, by definition and through its main agents—transnational corporations—will not be bound by any one nation, even the United States, and will operate so as to maximize profit (and minimize loss) by moving around the globe in its own distinct ways through such practices as transfer pricing, outsourcing, and tax alleviation. At the core of global commerce, it simply will not matter where a company is based.[8] Consensus, cooperation, and the rule of law will be hallmarks of this integrated global economy. Power will be defined along the lines of the best strategic alliances established and the power of brands to transcend single audiences and markets and attract continuing innovations in service. The raw media power, reach, and compelling content of communications, entertainment, and Internet companies will define the range of cultural power. English, however, has become the de facto official language of the new integrated digital global economy, and its unifying significance should not be discounted or forgotten for the written word, scientific research, financial dealings, and most powerfully, perhaps, as the lingua franca of the next generation, particularly on the Internet.

Ideology

Much has been said about the death of ideology resulting from the demise of Marxism-Leninism. Because the veneer of Marxist ideological belief held no great sway in the popular Russian mind anyway, it no longer incited belief or social cohesion. The ideological and moral aspect of the disappearance of communism on the global stage has been much overlooked. The reconstruction now taking place in the former centrally planned economies presupposes a radical shift of attitudes and core beliefs. New core ideas are still surfacing, as is the resurfacing of fundamentalism of a religious variety on nearly every continent. It has been nearly half a millennium since the world has known religiously grounded conflict. This time around, using communications networks, the ideologies will also be global in nature. They will often have ugly faces rooted in age-old forms of bigotry, terror, racism, and ethnic and religious rivalry.

Respect for freedom has replaced the void left by the death of ideology. With economic freedom, most of the world's markets are now more open to business: open to those ready to seize the opportunity presented by democratic capitalism. The globalization of economic integration we will continue to experience is due in part to the lure of liberal-participatory democracy and a Western definition of human rights, and in part to the power of consumer demand. People everywhere want goods and services to be available and affordable, even customized to meet their particular desires—all of which reinforces the power of marketing and distribution power to meet the global market.

The integrated global economy is demanding an entrepreneurial system, albeit with a human face, that respects personhood, cultures, and community. The record shows that the free-enterprise system alone creates economic and therefore social progress. The economic value created by commerce provides the resources for public-sector social services and security, as well as the resources for philanthropic and nonprofit services and culture. Human well-being requires this full range of resources and activities. The historic alternative to entrepreneurial commerce as an engine to fund human welfare, of course, is imperial conquest and pillage. The drivers of free markets are entrepreneurs cognizant of their social, global, ecological, and corporate responsibilities. The goal is that, for the first time in history, everyone can truly prosper. The role and responsibility of the United States, and particularly its defense of such a system, is the linchpin of this emerging system. As the only superpower and solution to regional conflict, the United States finds itself in a unique position: the engine of global economic growth, pacesetter for innovation and culture, and protector of the rule of law. In the past three decades, the United States has become the de facto arbitrator of nearly every serious dispute or armed conflict. Although hesitant at nation-building, the United States, post-9/11, has taken up the charge in earnest. American soft power is perhaps its greatest asset as the world seeks to mimic its popular culture and brand-name goods. Balancing hard power and soft power will prove difficult in the years ahead, as the war in Iraq has already shown.

The cultural revolution of the twenty-first century is too big to miss. Big corporate organizations of every stripe, from Coca Cola to Sony, are cashing in on it. The millennium has arrived, and we face a new world of opportunity. The changing demography boggles the mind. Progress now depends on our capability to live together in a multicultural world. The United States itself is increasingly diverse. Its melting pot and immigration history support the widest collection of cultures. In effect, the U.S. social order models the social and organizational order emerging as the most effective for dynamic growth in organizations—the open, permeable network with a streamlined core and targeted activities. If this is so, American civil society offers a model and lessons important to the flourishing of countries around the world, not because we seek to make the world like us but because core ideas implemented in America are structurally aligned with personal well-being. Modesty requires, of course, that we also note that the structure of American society remains a work in progress. The greatest challenge in the early twenty-first century is to improve our understanding of and sensitivity to traditions, cultures, religions, and generations different from our own: to take the human dimension seriously.

Rampant nationalism is being purged from the integrated global economy—but not without a fight. The world is a tapestry—of peoples, languages, religions, and histories—woven together to make one whole. Each part is distinct and yet rich in and of itself. Individuals, groups, nations, races, and regions will have to coexist and interact in the coming years at new levels of cooperation and interdependence. Economics is the common thread, and its transnational corporate actors are the very embodiment of the kinds of organization required to form another civilization, anchored more in tolerance than in exclusivity.[9] **The prospects for greater civility are grounded in a civic culture that is formed by civility. Civil societies are emerging around the world, shaped by notions of human flourishing and conditioned on the premise that private, public, and social sectors each have something unique to provide to the future.**

The new global reality also requires protection of endangered cultures as it protects endangered species, by avoiding situations in which one dominant, homogenized world culture operates to snuff out the diverse richness that has been built up over the centuries. As we come together in an integrated digital global economy, a countertrend will arise: to maintain distinctiveness. Companies and organizations would be wise to establish distinct marketing programs and services for distinct populations on each continent or in each subregion. Cyberspace is infinite; hence, that territory can be made available for continuous expansion to any and all groups and individuals, free from the constraints of physical reality or past territoriality.

We live together in a world that is held together by complex global financial, industrial, and information systems. Despite the fact that we are global neighbors, we are still characterized by real cultural differences and language, rooted in thousands of years of human undertaking. If we recognize each culture as a subsystem of a larger evolving global culture, it will be easier to survive, to prosper, and to flourish. It is a world of fewer regulations, greater decentralization, extensive privatization, expanded zones of private freedom, and, of course, economic integration. The state itself will still maintain power to ensure a system of justice and the rule of law but will no longer be the center of attention or the only power with the force to administer solutions. Nation-states themselves may in time be replaced or evolve into both smaller localized entities and larger regional communities. This phenomenon is well under way in Western Europe, Asia, and North America. The business, military, and social implications of these processes are indeed very far reaching.

One primary question of empowerment will be how the modern state, public corporations, and private entities interact in relation to other social institutions, such as families, schools, churches and other religious organizations, the arts, and voluntary organizations. Differentiated societies are producing a new philosophy embracing a more pluralistic, secularized world platform and an integrated global economy inside of which a diverse array of cultures, religions, and private interests are organized. Businesses are partnering with nonprofit organizations and with those who can help to create new markets as fully responsible societal leaders. We note the rise of corporate statesmanship and, in certain settings, the emergence of business-based political parties or advocacy, including candidates from business, with no prior political experience.

Strategic Factors

Columbus sought to find a strategic advantage by finding a shorter route to the Indies. His effort required years to complete. In the end, he did not find a shortcut to the East but something of even greater importance: the discovery of new continents. In our integrated global economy today and for the decades ahead, the major discoveries that rival Columbus's will be strategic shortcuts in the use of knowledge and time. For our new world, knowledge and time itself are the most important strategic factors—the measure both of things gained and of opportunities lost.

Further, we cannot afford for the discoveries of these new worlds to take years. Today, we cannot be satisfied, even if we travel at a supersonic speed, because the people of the world and their integrated economy can never be satisfied.[10] The sun never sets on the global economy and its demands and opportunities. Thirty years ago, 10 billion dollars crossed international borders every day. Today, 10 billion dollars cross international boundaries every second. This is just one sign of the vast appetite of the global economy and the exponential acceleration of pace it drives.

The allocation and management of these precious commodities—knowledge and time—will dominate the world whose threshold we are now crossing. Corporations spend much of their time and effort on improving cycle time, cutting inventories, and rationalizing or better managing their supply chains. The organizations we live in to bring about some semblance of order are still time-bound. Real-time, time-sensitive, overnight, just-in-time, all the time, 24/7—the great challenge, to quote a well-known corporate titan, is to do what we do today in half the time, tomorrow. In a faster and faster world of shortened cycle times, in which the processing of information becomes a cheaper and faster phenomenon every 18 months (Moore's Law), we face a situation of nearly unlimited bandwidth and ever-faster companies and organizations, where time to market can mean winner takes all.

Organizations of the future—corporate, social sector, governmental, and supranational—will affect and be affected by what Barbara Ward, the famous British economist and author, claimed were the "ideas that change the world."[11] The future world seemingly will be less organized, less state dominated, and less centralized than those before. It will nonetheless be formed as part of a whole yet still integrating global economy. The integration process itself, so much part and parcel of globalization, is likely to start and stop and will therefore prove to be somewhat uneven. Some groups will integrate more quickly than others. Still others will resist or even sabotage the developments and

progress we are experiencing all around us. Establishing an institution's or corporation's new services or business: customers,
mission focus, exploring the relationships of the social and market forces, competitive strategies, and investment opportunities
in a world pregnant with uncertainty and opportunity are the
hallmarks of a world full of future possibilities. Realizing such
global opportunity is a large undertaking, if not a daunting task.
The future is not one of stability but one of ongoing change.

Technology Advances and Humanity

With the advent of telematics—the combination of electronic
data processing and telecommunications—transmission of information related to the delivery of goods and services is more nearly reaching optimum efficiency. Electronic data interchange has
ushered in an age of "paperless trading." EDI produces significant savings when applied to global trade facilitation, administration, transport, and inventory control and also minimizes
paperwork and delays in the international movement of goods
and customs. Telematics and network technology integration are
saving billions of dollars for the smartest and most technologically advanced corporations. Most organizations in the future will
be part of interconnected networks on which they conduct business and form electronic communities. The impact of the Internet
and company intranets on logistics should not be underestimated across the entire supply chain. Advanced logistics utilizing the
most recent technologies are transforming the way business is
done. The mantra "better, cheaper, faster" is coming to reality,
fostered by technological advances.

The other key element driving technology in the digital global economy is the development of "global time information."
Global data flows have transformed markets and rendered con-
trols on its dissemination meaningless. This has resulted in
decentralization and a shortened scope for decision making.
Government leaders in the White House and presidential offices
everywhere in the world today watch uprisings on TV screens as
they occur. This makes elaborate information gathering, analysis,

and planning increasingly difficult for even the largest organizations. While events are simultaneously aired in living rooms around the world, details of the event are being faxed or e-mailed by instant messenger and web-blogs in real time, half a world away. New technologies often unify markets, requiring rapid responses and radically innovative thinking. In such a dynamic environment, information technology leverages both time and human resources. This is the reality of the world that technology is helping to create.

The historic emergence of Europe's single market over the past decades was in large part due to the interconnectivity of information. Information was also a key element in the transition from command economies to free-market economies in Eastern Europe, the Soviet Union, and, increasingly, throughout the developing or emerging world. This dynamic is irreversible, since a chip-driven, information-dominated economy is not built on concepts of central control. Technologically savvy industries have a number of interchangeable components that together make a new beehive out of complexity. James Botkin's book *Smart Business*, using the bee as the metaphor, develops a thesis about the wide net of alliances woven by multinational corporations using knowledge to create smart products and services.[12] This is the most likely future: literally, the knowledge business on a global basis. The research university is an integral part of this complex network, as universities partner with corporations to develop new intellectual property in a host of emerging technologies, ranging from nanotechnology to biotechnology and the life sciences. Although currently on the margin of this complex network, liberal arts colleges could be critical nodes that help to provide interpretation, cultural perspective, and clarity about ethical and human purposes for transactions in the global system.

The world today is akin to a series of local area networks that form a cybernetic wide area network, accessible through the World Wide Web. Being alone outside the loop is to be cut off from access to information. Such isolation will inhibit ability to think and to make informed decisions. If organizational plans are based on the reality of this integrated network, they have a better chance to prosper. Looking at the world as such a system renders more and more irrelevant the difference between industrialized and industrializing countries. Already we see flourishing software businesses in India, shared services locating in Ireland, call centers in Sri Lanka, and computer manufacturing in Taiwan or along the Mexican border with the United States. Perhaps, issues of *information have-nots* are as likely to cause social unrest in the future as political famines or dictatorship. To be part of the global network requires maximum adaptability. Such flexibility requires more deregulation, decentralization, and privatization. Those left outside the system find themselves in the backwaters, never able to fully catch up.

In the emerging technological and increasingly globalized digital world, organizations will not experience as much product competition as *systems competition.* Industrial-age competition was based on well-known price and quality competitiveness factors. Systems competition is much more complicated. Its decisive elements involve customer utility, methods of production, and the ability to quickly distribute bundled or unbundled packaged or even electronic goods and services. To excel at systems competition will demand greater logistics optimization. In short, competition will require hardware already loaded with software—with as many options as desired by the end user.

In this new world, some will be hurt; others, not included. Dislocation is always trying and painful, especially for the individuals and communities most affected. Already, we see the start of this with the arrival of Net-based businesses and the integration of information technology into every facet of life, leisure, and work. Disintermediation and outsourcing are real phenomena with real social costs.

Web-based technologies allow organizations to emulate or substitute with computer systems almost the entire physical-world experience between buyer and seller. Retailers use the technology to engage customers and facilitate transactions. Corporations embrace the Web as a platform to automate their business-to-business procurement processes. Aggregators use the Web to bring together multiple sellers and buyers in electronic marketplaces. Indeed, there are endless opportunities for those who have the foresight to build the best knowledge infrastructures and knowledge communities.

Corporations and universities are increasingly willing to pay for performers who can lead breakthroughs and create value for shareholders and stakeholders. This has implications for human resources and the sourcing of global organizations. Business and nonprofit leaders are designing this infrastructure to draw them closer to their markets, to avoid political and other risks, and to sidestep regulatory hurdles. Underlying all these changes is advancing technology—at a pace and with far greater ramifications than at any previous time in the human saga.

The humanities are, if willing, large beneficiaries of these new technologies. Digital libraries and enhanced communication and dissemination of content using rich, new media can and should benefit all they do. As part of the larger and global community, they need to be part and parcel of the changed experience, not Luddites castigating it or stuck in some distant past. There is a very important role for humanities to play in the transformation to technological civilization. By showing the history of science and the effect of technology on the human experience, they can hasten the acceptance of new technologies. They can also show the risks and downside of rapid adaptation. **The humanities need to befriend technological change and tame its darker side with humanism. Technology enhances the prospects for human flourishing, and the humanities comprehend and record that fact, including the all-important human dimension.**

Notes

1. Gerald Ross, *Toppling the Pyramid* (Boston, MA: Little, Brown, 1992).
2. Timothy Yeager, *Institutions, Transition Economics and Economic Development* (Boulder, CO: Westview Press, 1999).
3. Michael Wolff, *BurnRate.* (New York: Simon & Schuster, 1999).
4. Kevin Kelly, *Out of Control* (London: Fourth Estate, 1994).

5. Francis Fukuyama, *The End of History and the Last Man* (New York: Free Press, 1992).
6. Samuel Huntington, *The Clash of Civilizations and the Remaking of World Order* (New York: Simon & Schuster, 1998).
7. Thomas Barnett, *The Pentagon's New Map* (New York: Putnam, 2004).
8. Peter Calow, *Controlling Environmental Risks* (New York: Wiley, 1997).
9. James O'Toole, *Leading Change* (San Francisco: Jossey-Bass, 1997).
10. David Ulrich, *Organizational Capacity* (New York: Wiley, 1996).
11. Barbara Ward, *Five Ideas That Change the World* (New York: Norton, 1959).
12. James Botkin, *Smart Business* (New York: Free Press, 1999).

4

Renewing the Links of the Humanities to Personal Liberty, Creativity, and the Pursuit of Happiness

A ROUND THE WORLD, individuals, communities, regions, and nations struggle to respond to the scope, speed, and meaning of change. This is the great issue of the day. The key drivers of this change include the emergence of smart technologies, the exponential growth of knowledge, globalization, the worldwide spread of democracy, and, increasingly, religious awareness and critique. These forces connect us with one another and with people around the globe in unprecedented new ways that both accelerate and amplify the impact of change. This new level of connectivity and interdependence makes cultural, human, and civic issues more and more critical. Indeed, although the humanities are not front and center in public awareness and affairs today, **the humanities, rethought and reenergized, could become the keystone to hold together the converging forces of globalization, smart technology, the explosion of knowledge, and the intersection of different cultures and religions.**

Experience of this change should challenge our ready-at-hand categories; it confronts us with more puzzles and concerns than we have language to express. Acknowledging the difficulty of description is critical now, because the change under way is so deep and vast. Here is where the humanities are critical resources. With their breadth of analytical tools and perspectives that spans religion, ethics, law, politics, philosophy, history, languages, and knowledge of cultures and heritage, the humanities offer a uniquely varied set of interpretative frameworks. Further, as the oldest set of formal human knowledge and theory, stretching from the prehistory religious views around the world, the humanities also embody the most historically comprehensive array of interpretive frameworks. In this sense, the humanities are the historiography of meaning. This historic and intellectual variety, flexibility, and depth are important to bring to bear on our present situation.

The categories and terms selected at times of deep, paradigmatic change are essential parts of shaping and determining the direction of the change as it unfolds. In these situations, description is destiny. Hence, a first step in giving shape to the unfolding change is to acknowledge the presence of a genuine mystery at the outset. We must acknowledge the uncertainty and unknown dimension of our situation and acknowledge the deeply creative work needed to find descriptions that are generative and productive. In the face of the current upheaval, the temptation is to use explanations and categories that are all too readily available. The media, politicians, celebrities, academics, and religious leaders currently rush to judgment to apply familiar rationales. By doing so, they put new wine in old bottles. Explanations of events that come too quickly and with too much moral certainty are likely to be misguided. Our challenge is to look below the surface of current language and description, which is already threadbare with its familiarity, to find the deeper current of events—the deeper direction of change—and to find a navigable course in these deeper currents. The rich texture of description and conceptual variety in the humanities can help us chart, or map, these deeper currents.

Experience with major cultural and intellectual shifts teaches that beginning points are critical. "In my beginning is my end," as T. S. Eliot poetically phrased it. What we choose as beginning points, as basic "facts," and as a sequence of events are selected to define an emerging frame of reference. These facts and this frame of reference must bear within its core a moral and grounded compass, a true north, an innate guide that can sustain ever more productive next steps and interpretation. The world is ripe for a shift in meaning.

The following passage from *The Gutenberg Elegies* provides one level of perspective for understanding today's global change from the vantage of personal experience:

> In my lifetime, I have witnessed and participated in what amounts to a massive shift—a wholesale transformation. Primarily, human relations have been subjected to a warping pressure that is something new under the sun. Those who argue that history is change, that change is constant, are missing the point. Our era has seen an escalation of the rate of change so drastic that accommodation has been short-circuited. The advent of the computer, and the astonishing sophistication achieved by our electronic communications media, has together turned a range of isolated changes into something systematic. Since World War II, we have stepped collectively out of an ancient and familiar solitude and into an enormous web of imponderable linkages. We have created the technology that not only enables us to change our basic nature, but is making such change all but inevitable.[1]

The contrast the author draws between the modes of awareness represented by the "ancient, familiar solitude" of traditional culture and the burgeoning awareness within a new "enormous web of imponderable linkage" captures a key dimension of the challenge we face today as we try to create a new cultural understanding of this change and thus to rethink the humanities. The tension referenced in an earlier chapter between the Islamic world and the secular and technological world is really a point of inflection between the lived world of ancient solitudes, with their traditional, often religiously grounded cultures, and the emerging lived world of global connection, continuous learning, innovation, and dynamic, flexible, and permeable social structures. This is a key personal and cultural inflection that merits study.

Culture at a Crossroad: Socratic Engagement or Cartesean Detachment

The situation of culture and the humanities, too, can be understood from this perspective. The humanities, as they have evolved to date, represent a culture of "ancient solitudes." Because of assumptions made several hundred years ago in shaping the scientific, philosophical, and cultural foundations of modern culture, the humanities were regrounded and reoriented in solitary reflection. Descartes, traditionally recognized as the founding figure of modern thought, demonstrates this redirection in the *Meditations on First Philosophy,* both in the ideas developed and in the setting. Descartes begins his investigations by physically retreating from society. Isolated in his room and wrapped in the covers of his bed (an archetypical modern symbol running from Descartes to Proust), Descartes begins to doubt everything he purports to know from experience, society, and history (all part of the public realm of knowledge) in order to recreate the world from his own self-evident ideas and reasoning. There is a triple solitude and self-reference here: the personal solitude of Descartes in his room, separated from society; the solitude of private reflection; and the requirement that any acceptable idea arising in this reflection should meet the sole criterion of being self-evident. Thus, solitude is not simply a conducive setting for thought; it is also a criterion of truth, since the only source of validity accepted by Descartes is self-evidence. In similar fashion, Montaigne famously withdrew from the world into the privacy of his library for reading, reflection, and writing. In this model, being human is identified with a separate realm of elevated thought and experience derived from the arts, history, literature, and private reflection. Human awareness is grounded, in this view, in forms of awareness that take us out of everyday awareness, through historical reflection, poetic or artistic experience, detached philosophical analysis, or some other rigorously "other" form of consciousness.

Now, like traditional societies facing change, the humanities have also adopted a voice primarily of regret and lament. Change of almost any sort is viewed principally as loss, and the path into the future tends to be seen as a path of increasing dehumanization within the field today. The humanities have developed a specialized expertise for cataloguing the losses produced by change. The creative task of articulating a vision for a positive human future and designing a new context through which to expand human well-being and happiness as a result of change is not widely embraced by humanists. But today, the explosion of new ideas and rapid global change has put the voice of humanities, as a voice of ancient solitude and lament, on the sideline of life, not at its center.

In more recent times, entry into primitive and non-Western cultural experience and thought continues this concept that authentically human awareness must be grounded in an awareness that is not "mainstream," or everyday. In this view, to become fully human is to move from everyday experience and into a realm of elevated and/or different experience. Although today, the elevated awareness supported by "high" culture is viewed with some skepticism, the cultivation of nontraditional modes of awareness for different ethnic, social, and gender groups continues the tradition of the modern project to bifurcate experience into the realm of enlightened, authentic experience (which is detached) and the experience of daily life. The activities of everyday life, in this view, pull us away from the privileged space of detachment and make us less human. "The world is too much with us," as Wordsworth put it. Commerce, politics, marriage, everyday affections and sentiments, and obligations are categorically different from and less than the "human" realm of private reflection, reading, nonmainstream or countercultural experience, and high intellectual and aesthetic experience.

An alternative model is provided by Socrates. Socrates, although also committed to the pursuit of happiness, truth, and authentic experience, placed himself at the center of the market-place and in the center of everyday life and activity. Through dialogue and engagement, Socrates served as both a catalyst and a bridge between the everyday life of the community and the events of high intellectual discovery and élan. In the Socratic model, to become fully human requires active engagement in the community and in life. The humanities are not withdrawn but infused through commerce, politics, marriage, and everyday affections and activities as informing principles. Thomas Jefferson placed a model of engaged, enlightened citizenship at the very core of the American experience. It shaped his view of the past and the future; as he observed in a letter, "I believe more in the dreams of the future than in the histories of the past." In line with this perspective, a Socratic model of the humanities is constructive and oriented to the future rather than to the past.

Hence, we are at a crossroads, with two models of the humanities and two possible philosophical viewpoints toward change, and the future before us. The modern era is over. The high detachment of modern culture bifurcated experience and led to the marginalization of the humanities. We remain in a transitional, liminal state, between the modern and the new global culture that is emerging around us. The urgent challenge and opportunity of our time is to rediscover a genuine, affirmative voice—a Jeffersonian voice—for the humanities in expanding the pursuit of happiness and human flourishing. This would require a new humanities orientation that does not start by denying the value of everyday human life, business activity, politics, and the values of mundane life. Instead, it would be an outlook that embraces the everyday world and helps to inspire it with hope and intellectual adventure. In this time of great change, we wonder again about the means to create leadership for freedom around the world; we wonder again about the methodology of productive, free inquiry and the shape and possible integration of knowledge; and we wonder afresh about the means of sharing deeply meaningful experience across and within a diverse, global cultural tapestry.

What Is at Stake?

The original links of the humanities to personal and political liberty, innovation, liberal learning, and the pursuit of happiness need to be clarified in order for the humanities and culture to play a substantial, constructive role with current global forces of change. This is not a matter solely of academic and cultural importance. Given the scope of changes around the world and the increasingly critical part that human innovation, character, and cultural interdependence play, the meaning and thrust of the humanities must be a matter of concern for corporate, government, educational, and nonprofit leaders as well. The stakes are too high for the direction of the humanities to be set aside by the social sectors at the forefront of much of today's change agenda.

The deep sources of human creativity and social capital are embedded in the genetic code of the humanities. Yet over time, more and more leaders and more and more citizens have lost the ability to "read" this deep code. The result is a potential loss of the wellsprings of creativity. As James Billington noted in the foreword to this book, some of the more creative periods of American influence have been shaped by corporate, political, and educational leaders who had a liberal education and deep understanding of religious, philosophical, political, and cultural issues. A new generation of humanist leaders is urgently needed today.

The humanities will not simply renew themselves. Change will require critique, dialogue, and rethinking. Business, government, foundation, educational, and civic leaders will need to join academics in this discussion to challenge assumptions and build a new consensus. A contemporary renewal and rethinking of the humanities also needs a grounding in the original impulses and inspiration that led to their creation. Leaders from every social sector need to understand these founding ideas and impulses in order to reconnect with them as sources of action today. Therefore, an overview of the origins of the humanities and liberal education is offered in this chapter. In the sections that follow, we try to explain and exemplify links between the liberal arts and freedom.

Origins of the Humanities

In the West, the humanities were born in the early Greek democratic communities in response to the need to cultivate leadership for democratic life. From this concern, the polis created a need for teachers and learning, which led to the creation of the first academic institutions in the West and to the core outline of the liberal arts and the curriculum in the Academy and the Lyceum. In response to the growing body of ideas and continuous reflection created through the academies, works of art and broader cultural and civic orders and institutions evolved.

At the heart of the humanities is the idea that personal knowledge is the source of freedom, civic culture, and the pursuit of happiness. "Know thyself" is the enduring Socratic concept. The humanities are dedicated to the notion that knowledge has a liberating and humanizing purpose over and above its factual and practical content. In this sense, all knowledge and all learning are intended to have a humanistic purpose. Through liberating acts of knowledge, people come to understand themselves in the cosmos and hence grow into the full dimensions of being human.

Since the times of Parmenides and Empedocles, individuals seeking to live a fully human life through the liberating achievement of knowledge have struggled with the conflicting pulls of private and public freedom. The struggle is inscribed in the very origins of the liberal arts, in the founding experiences and events of the effort to be human by means of the effort to know. The discovery of knowing as a means of freedom is surely one of the most momentous in history. The discovery that through knowledge, one may be liberated from the confines and prejudices of a particular time and locale and be empowered to act on a more expansive plane is an original and continuing initiation into culture. "The mind is its own place," as Milton's Satan declares, "And can make of itself a Heaven of Hell, a Hell of Heaven."[2]

At some point, if we are true to ourselves, we all come to this discovery. From the struggles of countless individuals in small towns everywhere to the struggles of an Einstein who cannot bend to established academic routines, the story expands to include us all. The public acknowledgment of such freedom of mind and the public allowance for its multiple expressions in different individual lives are what we cherish as civilization. Civilization is the continuing ceremony that permits, acknowledges, and enriches individual acts of liberating thought. The celebration of a canon and other monuments of civilization, often critiqued today as instruments of authority and dominance, is intended to serve as public witness and as mile posts to the inner freedom of conscience and the individual mind at the very foundation of society.

How are these instances of liberating insight to be described? By their nature, they seem to defy description and to resist limitations of disciplinary boundaries. Archimedes in his garden, so entranced by the unraveling puzzle and beauty of a complex proof that he refused to stop his writing while soldiers beat at the front gate and so, still at work, must be carried with his table by his servants, is but an example. Or Socrates standing for hours, deep in thought, is another case. Various great mathematicians, including contemporary British mathematician Roger Penrose, who created the mathematics used to describe the big bang theory of the origin of the universe, describe these experiences of "being in the world yet not of the world" with such regularity that we must concede that higher mathematics and logic are activities specially suited to the mind's greatest liberties.

But the experiences are not restricted to mathematics and metaphysics. Probably each of us has experienced an artistic performance that created a similar category of awareness not only for ourselves individually but also for an audience. The arts have the distinct advantage of leading us individually to an inner freedom while at the same time enacting the experience in public and with communal participation. We have been present for opera performances when a particular aria has brought the entire audience to a common point of almost breathless expectation and heightened awareness. Each time we experience a dance as dance, we move beyond the scattered movements to something larger, an achieved whole that Susan Langer has called a "virtual entity."[3] The "dance" never exists—there are only momentary movements—but the form of the dance emerges like a stroboscopic effect, and by seeing it, we experience the world like a mathematician who sees a proof.

A poem or a work of literature may be grasped in such a way. Rilke said that no one could "look" at a Greek torso without hearing the command, "change thyself." The work of art is not the created artifact but the work we perform in transformative response. Thoreau wrote in *Walden* that "it is a wonderful thing to paint a picture or carve a statue, and so make some thing beautiful. But to affect the quality of the day, which morally we can do, is the greatest of the arts."[4] The greatest of the arts—the liberal arts—is to achieve an inner freedom and transformation of such integrity and power that our own experience and action affect the quality of the day. We are transformed and transforming. This is one way to enter into the liberating freedom of the mind through art and reflective thought.

Or, standing at Gettysburg or Normandy, we may be transported not only back in time to those battles but also to an awareness of the similarity and simultaneity of all the battles of history, and the future. In these moments, we experience time itself, not simply as the passing moment but as an accumulated presence with the fullness of Proust's novel. Or as T. S. Eliot put it in the opening lines of *The Four Quartets*:

> Time present and time past
> Are both perhaps present in time future,
> And time future contained in time past.
> If all time is eternally present,
> All time is unredeemable.
> What might have been is an abstraction
> Only in a world of speculation.
> What might have been and what has been
> Point to one end, which is always present.[5]

The mind's grasp of time may become linked with profound religious insight; or, in the passing and loss of time, the love of two people for each other may achieve a special tenderness and height. Mathematics, art, ethics, history, science, religious epiphany, love, memory, and loss—the range of experiences from which we may depart for a transforming and liberating knowledge seems endless. Robert Frost described the experience with humor and precision:

> Tell Tissaphernes not to mind the Greeks:
> The freedom they seek is by politics,
> Forever voting and haranguing for it.
> The reason artists show so little interest
> In public freedom is because the freedom
> They've come to feel the need of is a kind
> No one can give them—they can scarce attain—
> The freedom of their own material:
> So, never at a loss in simile,
> They can command the exact affinity
> Of anything they are confronted with.
> This perfect moment of unbafflement,
> When no man's name and no noun's adjective
> But summons out of nowhere like a jinni.
> We know not what we owe this moment to.
> It may be wine, but much more likely love—
> Possibly just well-being in the body,
> Or respite from the thought of rivalry.
> It's what my father must mean by departure,
> Freedom to flash off into wild connection.
> Once to have known it, nothing else will do.
> Our days all pass awaiting its return.
> You must have read the famous valentine
> Pericles sent Aspasia in absentia
>
> For God himself the height of feeling free
> Must have been His success in simile
> When at sight of you He thought of me. [6]

How are such experiences of the freedom Frost called "unbafflement" to be described? Note how Frost struggles to do so, moving from what the experience is not—not baffled; a lack of rivalry; departure, not being where you are; drunkenness, or loss of controlled awareness; not inspiration—but rather the body's well-being, perhaps love, something from a source we do not know. Especially today, we often hesitate to affirm a source and keep to the discipline of negative theology.

What is the character of experience when, after reading Spinoza, the strange and disconnected axioms and corollaries snap together and the Ethics leaps out from its formal puzzle like a hologram of Princess Leia from *Star Wars*, whole and animated, speaking to us like a friend and yet absolutely separated from us and untouchable? What is the feeling when our minds enter so deeply into the Platonic dialogues or a play by Shakespeare that the next word on the page seems as familiar as our next thought—the very thing we would have said—as the mind flows like water over the contours of the work, a perfect dressage of thought and text?

How do we describe the experience of suspended lightness and grounded support that coalesce in the transition of the third movement of the Beethoven String Quartet Opus 131, when the tortured, slow grinding of chords resolves at the quietest moment into a simple C-major chord played in unison by the four instruments and then suddenly shifts into a quick, joyful melody? What do we know at that moment but the freedom of the mind to flash off into wild connections, as Frost said, to leap from pain to joy without transition? The solution of the logical or mathematical problem is the same wild leap into a connection, a breaking away from what is limited by confusion to the enacted freedom of solution and the grace of unbafflement.

Standing in front of a Vermeer painting, how is our experience changed simply by looking at a woman who does not see us but absorbs herself in her letter as we absorb ourselves in her attention? Mihaly Csikszentmihalyi describes these moments as "flow experience," experiences when time melts away, and we are fully and completely absorbed in our own activity or attention. At such times, we merge with our surroundings and ourselves in a larger unity, which does not permit our reflective awareness or analysis.[7]

All these varied types of transformed awareness have been given a central place in our culture as definitive of being human.

Such experience has also been enshrined in the East in a culture, literature, art, and social order both complex and foreign, as well as impossible to summarize. When Socrates said that "the unexamined life is not worth living," we have come to understand that he meant that life is not worth living devoid of the "freedom to flash off into wild connections," a life devoid of religious epiphany, scientific discovery, mathematical intuition, remembrance of past time, artistic experience, or the self-losing experience of love. A life without these experiences is truly not human.

The humanities collect and transmit these moments and strive to keep open the space in which they occur. The liberal arts as a curriculum of study in schools and universities aim to pass an extensive collection of transfigured experiences from generation to generation and so to provide as many authentic types of liberating knowledge as possible to the diverse and unpredictable impulses of youth. Teaching these experiences is the heart of the liberal arts as they have been taught since the time of the Greeks. "It is this millennial continuity," George Steiner has written, "which may be our principal inheritance and the axis of what we call, always provisionally, western culture."[8]

The possibility for such experience is latent and inscribed in the fabric of everyday awareness. Variety, complexity, beauty, and design are all there abundantly. Yet experience is incomplete. The act of describing takes one deeper into the experience. The addition of a human intention and framework—acts that elude detail—in fact add to the depth of engagement. Integrating into the fullness of the present is not possible without the excision of form accomplished by the mind.

Despite the difficulty of describing these moments of knowing, it is undeniable that people have experienced them, in one form or another, throughout history and in the present. But in acknowledging their existence, how do we evaluate them? What is the proper value to assign to each experience? What is appropriate to do in response by way of building institutions, customs, and laws to preserve and promote these experiences? What investment of resources is appropriate, given the range and pinch of needs? Moreover, what are the ontological implications of these experiences? What, if anything, do these experiences reveal to us about the real world, about the nature of reality itself? Do they mean something beyond the moment in which they occur? Are they a part of the world, part of its very fabric, or are they anomalies and aberrations, something merely subjective in the mind? One set of questions takes us to ethics and politics; the other set, into metaphysics and theology.

The question of value returns us to the heart of the original dilemma of the humanities and liberal arts. The experience of liberating knowledge stands at odds with both the reality and activities of the community and the world we know and share with others. The dilemma starts in comedy. Thales, the first known philosopher-scientist in the West, falls into a well while looking at the stars. The whole town in which Thales lives is wildly amused by his accident and sees a lesson in it. Later, Thales is comically unembarrassed when a delegation of nobles finds him covered in soot, cleaning his fireplace—"There are gods even in the fireplace," Thales observes, unashamed.

The freedom discovered by the mind is a freedom set apart from the freedom of the community. This is part of its charm. As Frost clearly notes in the poem quoted earlier, the freedom sought by the artist is different from the freedom of the state. Frost belittles the freedom of public harangue and voting. The customs, ideas, and actions of the public clearly occupy a place of lesser importance than the customs, ideas, and actions of the artist, who knows how to "flash off into wild connection." Departure, again as Frost notes, is the key. The liberated mind departs. It leaves the community in order to find itself and once found, refuses to be bound by the community in the same way as in the past. To the one who departs, departure is delightful, liberating, but to the community, departure is suspicious and a source of envy and wounded pride. Departure and resentment thus become linked by the original liberation of the mind. This rupture appears final; how can it ever be overcome by either side? A possible resolution is the creation of a new set of relations that create a new community of free minds and hearts. To create such a community would it be to create a new political reality, a new polis, or republic—a *Republic of Letters*, or a republic of historical men and women—that is the question. The academic community exists to live out this prospect and struggles with its relation to the broader community beyond the academy's walls.

The educated mind is the firmest source of personal freedom. As liberating acts of understanding became a definitive category of experience and as narratives of their discovery and discoveries proliferated, they began to develop a critical mass, shape, and sequent meaning. Plato's Academy and Aristotle's Lyceum, followed by other schools, became organized communities dedicated to pursuing inner freedom through the creation of knowledge. As we know from history, there were even early attempts to change the course of history outside the academies, but these were unsuccessful.[9] So, a growing community dedicated to the pursuit of inquiry and knowledge came into being and began to develop institutional stature. These new communities of study formed the basis for the university and schooling system. Today, the modern university, which is heir to this tradition, is increasingly central to the economic future of companies, governments, and communities. Communities set apart for research and learning are major economic drivers and sources of talent.

In place of isolated experiences of insight, a body of texts and cultural artifacts began to be created through the budding academies and the broader educated culture they spawned. These books, artworks, and cultural expressions were created in such a way as to refer to one another in extended conversation, allusion, argument, and surprising connections over time. If to be free is to know, then to know came to mean to inscribe a growing body of cultural and intellectual references anchored by literature and culture. The core medium for transmitting this knowledge and freedom was dialogue convened around texts: in other words, the culture of the liberal arts was at its core literate.

To write and to read a poem like Dante's *Divine Comedy* is to live in a virtual construct of great complexity. Each word and image in the poem evokes an echo from prior poems along a continuum of allusion and quotation. To be literate, within the liberal arts tradition, is of course more than a matter of decoding words or reading quantities of texts. A 2004 National Education Association study on literacy in America, which simply quantified basic literacy and numbers of books, magazines, and newspapers read, examines a form of literacy that would have had little or no significance to humanistic studies. The literacy of the older tradition, today almost totally lost, is literacy of implied allusion, a literacy between the lines. The literate, liberally trained, and liberated mind experiences the negative spaces and implicit structure of thought. This implicit meaning is sustained like a vast suspension bridge over time and over continually evolving literary forms and genres. Recognition of this implicit "text," this other world "flashing off into wild connection," sustains the freedom of the mind against the limitations of time and place and opens a broad field of playful creation and variety to the educated imagination, the content of which is human experience and thought itself. This vast field of codified experience thus expands and enriches the experience of each individual who comes to know it.

In nature, there is a condition in which water changes continuously and so rapidly between the state of being a liquid and a gas that it becomes luminous. This condition is called *critical opalescence.* This physical state is a suitable metaphor for the educated imagination. The educated imagination exists in a state of critical opalescence as the experience of one creation, one poem, one philosophical concept, one symphony; one mathematical proof evokes a continuous shimmering vibration, echo, and transformation in the light of prior creations and the implied possibilities of new ones. Today, these internal connections appear to most people to be external ornamentations that require pages of footnotes to explain. But this is because we no longer live in the enacted performance of our culture. The connections are not immediately felt. We no longer experience culture in active and alert response but look at it from outside, using footnotes and descriptive museum labels to inform us of what we are looking at. The loss of the ability to live freely and playfully within culture is what once was called illiteracy. The academic community, and the liberal arts specifically, dedicated itself to the opposite: to literacy. That is, the liberal arts community was a special community dedicated to living culture, to embodying culture, and to transmitting it from generation to generation through example, reading, dialogue, and creative response.

The Enlightenment, Romantic, and Postmodern Variations: Sources of Victimhood

Since the eighteenth century, this academic culture in the West took two different paths: the path of Enlightenment and the path of Romanticism. The Enlightenment posited a privileged position to the activity of reason in comprehending the world and human experience. Whereas the bulk of humanity may blunder along in darkness, Enlightenment thinkers envisioned a new, cosmopolitan community—a "Republic of Letters," as Leibniz and others of his day called it—dedicated to the rule of reason. The special status of rational thought, a totally autonomous reason, they believed, stood apart from the main currents of history and provided a privileged and pure perspective from which to view the world. Against the claims of the Enlightenment, the romantics argued that reason distorted reality and that the privileged point of view belonged to purity of sentiment and authenticity. Authentic being—rooted directly in nature and the sentiments and later in imagination and even later in existential clarity and decisiveness—provided privileged access to knowing and being in the world.

Postmodernism today has trumped both critiques, pointing out that neither reason nor love is free from power structures, and so neither is pure and privileged. To reason is to categorize, to order, to name, and so to exclude something. Likewise, love and other modes of authenticity covertly or openly enact relations of dominance and subordination. Unmasking the charades of reason and authenticity emerges as a core activity of the postmodern academic liberal arts community, along with initiation into the cultures and views of various ethnic and gender groups. But a community and enterprise founded on the idea of "liberating" acts of knowing does not provide liberation; rather, it now finds itself cataloguing inevitable and infinite methods of enslavement and victimhood.

Perhaps this is cause enough to remember the originating experiences and purposes of the humanities. The enterprise of creating and guiding a human future with vast new tools, networks, and information at our disposal is surely comparable in scale to the challenge of creating democracy out of tribalism in ancient Greece. The opportunity is ripe with unprecedented potential good and unprecedented potential danger. That is to be expected; the scale of risk and the scale of good may be equal. Wisdom, an ancient and pressing notion, is necessary, and that wisdom continues latent within the depths of the humanities and the great achievements of the academic community. Rethinking this tradition will require significant reevaluation of assumptions and radical reform.

A Clean Sweep: The Irrelevance of the Humanities and the Future as Scientism

When Descartes split reality in half, he hardly expected the long-range consequences of his project on culture and religion. To Descartes, a devout Catholic, the division of reality into the physical world of extended bodies in space and time and the mental world of consciousness and thought seemed self-evident. Of course, he did not pause to reflect on why this idea seemed self-evident. He did not acknowledge the deep heritage of medieval ontology that lay behind his own categories. Compared with the medieval analysis of Being as a complex, hierarchical structure, Descartes' analysis was a breathtaking simplification. Cutting through all the complexities and ambiguities of Being described in medieval science, Descartes concluded that existence was simple and uniform with only two aspects: mind and body. The spirit of modernism is largely summarized in this step: modernism represents ways to sweep away the past, understood as a source of superstition and fables, using methods of thinking that emphasize simplicity, uniformity, and self-evident ideas that any rational individual can acknowledge. Modernism, as outlined by Descartes and his followers, is equivalent to simplification and radical newness.

Over time, this division of reality did become accepted as common sense. Further, this division implied a new alignment of activities and studies. The new, "modern" sciences took shape around Descartes' category of *res extensa,* and as a result, measurement became the key to scientific method. Whereas classical and medieval science had allowed for multiple methodologies and studies, modern science proposed a single scientific method of quantification as the only genuine way to know the world outside our own thoughts and feelings. The implications of this idea were applied first to physics, with Sir Isaac Newton setting the standard with the *Principia Mathematica,* and over the course of time, any discipline of study aspiring to the level of science adopted mathematics and measurement as the key tool of analysis.

This shift in method was also supported by the idea that the mind and consciousness constituted its own, independent field of knowledge and study, with its own distinct methods. That is, the Cartesian model posited two fields of knowledge: the physical world outside the mind and the mental world known in consciousness. Over time, a variety of approaches to understanding consciousness were conceived; most notably, German Idealism and Romanticism proposed a range of possible understandings of Mind that culminate in the idealism of Hegel. Most of the great works of modern literature, philosophy, art, history, and theology were created under the influence of Idealism and Romanticism to develop studies of human consciousness comparable and equal to the sciences.

Following Descartes' division of reality, Western culture ultimately split into two movements and intellectual camps: a growing community of "scientists" dedicated to studying the physical world and extending the use of scientific method to ever wider fields of inquiry and, on the other hand, a community of "humanists" who studied the world of human consciousness, value, and meaning. C. P. Snow referred to this divide with his famous essay on "The Two Cultures."[10] As we know, this split proved unstable. Inevitably, rivalry developed between the claims of the two camps over a wide array of phenomena. First, the humanists claimed to speak from a deeper and more comprehensive truth and, in the form of Idealism and Romanticism, argued that the "external world" was really simply a manifestation of the mind or imagination—the mind of man and the mind of God, or to shift toward Romanticism, the human imagination and the Spirit inspiring nature.

Through most of the eighteenth and nineteenth centuries, humanism, expressed through some version of Idealism or Romanticism, was the dominant cultural force; this intellectual dominance supported the claims of religion, art, history, politics, and the humanities generally to intellectual primacy and access to a "higher truth." In this view, the human meaning created through the mind and culture exists in a separate, higher realm that cannot be disturbed by science. This is a recurrent theme in the religious, artistic, and philosophical work throughout these centuries and well into the middle of the twentieth century. (It still occurs today when people argue that religious truth exists in one box and scientific truths exist in a separate box, as though this conceptual dualism made sense.) At the same time, the sciences continued to grow and to apply new scientific methods and mathematics to more and more phenomena. The sciences became more assertive about the scope of their work and critical of the assumptions that culture represented a higher truth. Tension between the claims of science and the claims of religion, art, and the humanities grew sharper and more intense.

The German philosopher Edmund Husserl felt this tension deeply and identified it as a major crisis in *The Crisis of European Sciences*, written in the 1930s. Husserl felt that a conceptually defensible connection between the sciences and human perception was critical to ensure the foundations of both science and humanism. Scientific method is grounded in observation, after all, which is conscious perception. Following Kant and Hegel's search for some "transcendental" categories linking mathematical science and experience, Husserl's "eidetic phenomenology" was intended to show the connections between the knowledge created in the natural sciences and the knowledge that arises in consciousness. Husserl proposed the creation of a new method—transcendental phenomenology—as a rigorous approach to ground and validate knowledge, at the same time avoiding either Idealism or Materialism. Twentieth-century Continental philosophy and phenomenology were born from this impulse to create a rigorous and valid form of humanism and to avoid reductive materialism.

The results of this ambitious intellectual diplomacy have not lived up to their aspirations. Like Idealism, phenomenology generated a host of incompatible variations on the theme—Husserl, Heidegger, Sartre, Merleau-Ponty, and others. While various phenomenologies proliferated, the natural sciences continued to grow and expand, fighting back the boundaries of humanistic studies. The primary battles were pitched over the nature of the mind, human action, politics, economics, sociology, and history. Humanists argued that the mind could not be reduced to the physical brain, that actions could not be reduced to stimulus and response, and that economics, sociology, and history all included irreducible "human" factors that could not be explained through mathematical analysis and models. Physicalists, on the other hand, argued that these claims were specious and empty and that, given enough time, consciousness would be reduced to biochemistry and action to physical causation and that scientific, predictive models of society, economics, and politics would replace subjective narratives and descriptions.

Today, the claims of humanism to a separate domain of knowledge equivalent to science have lost their power to persuade. Momentum, creativity, and energy are on the side of the sciences. As a result, the stories we tell about the future are tied largely to modern science. The outlines of this story are familiar, namely, that the future is defined by scientific advances and the steady retreat of religious, artistic, and humanistic claims to truth.

Intellectually, this implies that ideas about life having meaning and purpose must be abandoned in favor of an objective, scientific view of the universe as meaningless. (Or, in some cases, religious and humanistic views are permitted to exist in a separate conceptual box where their claims cannot conflict with the dominance of science on "real" knowledge and truth. This is a tenuous intellectual position.) Religion and traditional humanism are seen as incompatible with science, and hence social progress driven by science is measured by increasing secularism and agnosticism about traditional values and religiously grounded values. The future, thus, is about the retreat of religion and tradition in the face of advancing science and secularism. In the popular imagination, "scientific" humanism projects a future pluralistic society like that dramatized in the various versions of *Star Trek*. From a policy perspective, the highly secularized societies of Western Europe are seen as the vanguard of social progress. This is Cartesian modernism writ large—a clean sweep of history and tradition in favor of a future built on simple, universal, abstract reason. Is this story of the future still viable?

Postmodern Humanism: The Future as Victimhood

With the collapse of modern humanism's claims to a "higher truth" of either reason or feeling, another variation has developed as an alternative to scientific humanism. This postmodern humanism places the consciousness of diverse ethnic, gender, and countercultural groups and individuals in the privileged space formerly held by reason and feeling. Using categories of dominance and subordination as the primary analytical framework, postmodern humanism has developed a focus on exposing variations on exploitation and victimization. Taking to heart the idea that the humanities cannot make truth claims, postmodern humanism embraces a new form of relativism and diversity as ends in themselves.

This outlook has also been developed in response to a narrowing of the spiritual and intellectual sources that have fed past forms of humanism. In the twentieth century, economics, political science, social science, history, and even literature shifted, with varying degrees of success, from qualitative interpretation and Socratic dialogue to quantification and mathematical modeling in an effort to complete the Cartesian project of quantification. As a result, these disciplines have succumbed to a kind of social-scientization, in which humanity is seen as the product of forces over which it has no control. When being a human begins to mean being a victim of past circumstance or past historical injustice—to a drunken father or a racist ideology or a less than fair economic situation or a sexual condition—such description casts a spell of doom on the person and the group, thereby reinforcing failure, encouraging excuse, and putting issues past logic into a realm of culture-power politics.

To restore the humanities to a constructive role, we must recognize that victimhood is an intellectual dead-end. Victimhood as a critical and practical model paralyzes action and hope for the future. Until we can move away from defining human life through the lens of dominance, subordination, and victimhood, there will be little hope for what Eliot called culture as a way of life. There seems no room for forgiveness. This is certainly not to claim that there are no victims in the world or to say that there are no power structures. Rather, the claim is that these are distorting when used as universal categories to apply everywhere. Is the victimhood of every person, every group, not an enslavement to the past and to its abundant evils in a way that paralyzes true action and hope in some future good? Justice demands a righting of wrongs—of penalty and of retribution—but when society itself is defined as an unending series of victims in shrill irrationality set against one another, what comes of the whole? Is reconciliation ever an option?

Some have argued that had the Enlightenment understood that there could be no presumption of carryover from civilization to civility, from humanism to the humane, the springs of hope would have been staunched. Without some confidence that culture is a renewing source of hope and liberation, as our best product, what is there to live for? If we expect the worst in ourselves, it most certainly will be realized. George Steiner, among others, has argued that culture and humane action, literacy, and political impulse are in no necessary or sufficient correlation. But is he correct? We may be bewildered, confused, or as T. S. Eliot thought, forced to return to an earlier pessimism, a model of history whose logic derives from a postulate of original sin. Surely, no one can deny the barbarism of the modern era, the acts of the educated in all the technological certainties of horror. The inhuman actions of so-called cultured persons are perhaps the most disturbing. There may no longer be any innocence.

The homeless mind, a diminishment of territorial definitions, of sense of place, and the supposed death of God in modern culture have made modernity a kind of Hell on Earth. If we do not know who we are, where we came from, or where we are headed, have we not lost our bearings?

Are all our human achievements—all our great literature, profound knowledge, beautiful art, and rich religious traditions—for naught? What have we learned if all we have come to is a series of ongoing and ever louder, more violent objections to our fellow travelers, in an increasingly global and integrated setting? Can we get on with the next stage of human development? Will we see progress instead of decline? Can we celebrate human achievement and applaud cultural pluralism?

New Realities

New realities have begun to call the modern scientific narrative of the future and postmodern forms of humanism into question. These can be divided into two broad categories: the surprising resurgence of religion around the world and the emergence of new categories of scientific theory that break down the old divisions. Far from withering away as science and technology advance, religion is on the rise around the world today. Studies from the University of Pennsylvania show that Christianity is growing exponentially, especially in the Far East and Africa, as well as in the United States.

This phenomenon is a major anomaly for the modern narrative of the future. As seen in the response to the 2004 American election, the increasing strength of religion as a cultural and political force does not fit the model. The resistance of Islam to modernization is another, extreme example. With the collapse of communism and socialism, religion is emerging around the world as a formative social driver. Political, academic, and media leaders are at a loss to understand this phenomenon and struggle to find terms and explanations—without success. They can view the phenomenon of religious vitality only as backwardness, as ignorant resistance to the progress of science and modernism. The future is supposed to be about the abandonment of tradition and religion, not their resurgence. Drawing on the arguments of Thomas Kuhn in *The Structure of Scientific Revolutions*, we can predict that the modern paradigm of secularism and progress is being challenged by anomalies that cannot be accommodated but that are likely to lead to a deep revolution in thought.[11]

At the same time, new understandings are emerging in the sciences themselves. The picture of the universe we find in the most advanced scientific theories bears little resemblance to the intellectual assumptions and models of modern science. Modern science conceived a highly simplified form of physical existence defined by indivisible, atomic matter moving predictably through space and time. Contemporary physics has shown that "atoms," or indivisible particles of matter, do not in fact exist. Instead, the molecular and atomic worlds open up into a vast, complex world of subatomic particles and forces that interact in surprisingly complicated ways across distance and through probabilities. Quantum mechanics introduces indeterminacy into physics, much to Einstein's dismay, and whole new theories of chaos, cybernetics, systems, and strings reveal a model of physical existence of great complexity and variety. The complexity, convergent beauty, and multileveled structure of this new cosmology and physics suggest an opportunity for a new dialogue between religion and science, as well as the humanities. Contemporary cosmology and biology are also discovering a range of interesting convergence. The mapping of the human genome, the specific calibrations of the initial conditions of the big bang, and the growing understanding of how information acts on matter in cybernetic hierarchies (like software's relation to hardware) are creating a platform for a new relation of the sciences to religion.

The story is told of a professor who in teaching an introductory class in philosophy presented the case for "eliminative materialism" to the class as a demonstration of how science would replace religious understanding. In this view, religious terms are primitive forms of explanation that ultimately receive translation into clear scientific explanations. So "Zeus's thunderbolts" becomes "electrical discharge between the earth and ions in the atmosphere," "demon possession" becomes "mental illness," and the "soul" or "mind" becomes the "brain," as Watson, a codiscoverer of DNA affirmed in one of his last works. One of the students pointed out that this model of "eliminating" religion assumes that religious thought remains unchanged, whereas scientific thought evolves. What would happen, he asked, if we assumed that both religious thought and science evolve together?

Perhaps this is the challenge today in an increasingly religious world: to find new ways to listen to the claims of religion and to find common ground with the new nonreductive scientific models that are replacing modern science. Could a new Aristotelian project be conceived to forge a synthesis that combines the best of science with religious faith and so restore humanity to a meaningful role in the cosmos? In the light of new realities, why should we assume that scientific materialism and secularism are inevitable or desirable? Such a synthesis would also provide space for a deeper humanism and a broader, more humane social and political culture suited to provide intellectual foundations for the pursuit of happiness.

The ultimate marks of cultural transformation include a revitalized humanism and culture that have overcome the dichotomies and historical arrogance of the modern world. For most of history, religion has provided the primary narrative of the future; this changed only within the modern period. With the close of the modern period, transformation can be measured by an increasing awareness of a new narrative of the future, a narrative compatible both with religious experience and with science.

Notes

1. Sven Birkerts, *The Gutenberg Elegies: The Fate of Reading in an Electronic Age* (London: Faber and Faber, 1994), p. 15.
2. John Milton, *Paradise Lost* (Oxford: Oxford University Press, 1998).
3. Susan Langer, "The Dynamic Image: Some Philosophical Reflections on Dance," in *Problems of Art* (New York: Scribner's, 1957), pp. 1–12.
4. Henry David Thoreau, *Walden* (New York: Avenel Books, 1985).
5. T. S. Eliot, *Collected Poems 1909–1962* (New York: Harcourt, Brace and World, 1963), p. 175.
6. Robert Frost, "Hard Not to Be King," in *The Collected Poetry of Robert Frost* (New York: Henry Holt, 1969), p. 461.
7. Mihaly Csikszentmihalyi, *Flow: The Psychology of Optimal Experience* (New York: Harper and Row, 1990).
8. George Steiner, *Lessons of the Masters* (Cambridge, MA: Harvard University Press, 2003), p. 7.
9. J. M. Cooper and D. S. Hutchinson, eds., "Epistle 7," in *Plato Complete Works* (Cambridge, MA: Hackett Publishing, 1997).
10. C. P. Snow, *The Two Cultures* (Cambridge: Cambridge University Press).
11. Thomas Kuhn, *The Structure of Scientific Revolutions*, 3rd ed. (Chicago: University of Chicago Press, 1996).

5

Responding to Changing Ideas, Needs, and Demands: A New Humanistic Vision

T HE CURRENT SITUATION, with its dramatic pressures and unprecedented change, presents tremendous opportunities for the humanities to make a significant contribution to American culture and global civil society. Significant contribution, however, is contingent on a rigorous rethinking of the humanities as a framework for not only understanding the dramatically transformed vistas of knowledge arising in science, mathematics, and smart technologies but also analyzing and understanding religious awareness, which is expanding worldwide. Also needed is a new framework and methodology for cross-cultural analysis and understanding grounded in humanistic studies.

This claim may seem surprising to many who note signs of atrophy and decline in the liberal arts and humanities. Others may feel that such a constructive project cuts against the grain of established contrarian perspectives and critical-study approaches broadly practiced today. To participate in a constructive approach to the human future would require creative collaboration with science, technology, and economic forces and greater engagement with everyday life. There are those for whom such collaboration would mean the sacrifice of what is constitutive of humanities' critical awareness. Replacing reason and authentic feeling, postmodern resistance and critique of the entire range of the everyday world are today seen by many to be epistemologically and ethically privileged.

Such views and evidence of atrophy exist. However, the decline of vital energies into routine and scholastic neologism and the extreme distance between everyday life and critical awareness may be the sign of emerging transformation. In the nineteenth century, physics was declared a dead subject incapable of adding new knowledge to the body of law and proof achieved by Newton. Physics became a repetitive and imitative formalism, torn by minor sectarian controversies. By the end of the century, however, there were Maxwell, Poincare, and then Einstein. Thomas Kuhn presented this scenario in detail in his classic, *The Structure of Scientific Revolutions*.[1] Today, we stand on such a threshold of change. We are in a liminal condition, a borderland full of the shadows of the past and scattered light of the dawning future. In physical systems, the threshold of a new level of organization is characterized by increased repetitive activity and apparent chaos. Such a state supports the emergence of a new level of order. This is where we stand today: on the precipice of a new order.

An Agenda for New Ideas

In the context of the dramatic change sweeping the world, four topics stand out as new horizons requiring humanistic understanding and extensive creative work. Each is a major constructive enterprise that will require focused work by many scholars and institutions, from both academic and other sectors. Here, we must limit ourselves to identifying the horizons where work is needed and outlining a possible programmatic approach. The domains are the

1. epistemological integration of digital information systems and smart technologies into the arena of human thought and culture;

2. creation of a new topology of knowledge that overcomes disciplinary boundaries that are obstacles to creative intellectual work;

3. creation of new understandings of leadership and its responsibilities in the light of social networks and new organizational functions and norms;

4. creation of a positive definition and role for what is now called the "nonprofit," or "nongovernmental," social sector, consistent with a revised understanding of the functions of the public and private sectors in a global, knowledge-based society/economy.

Chapters 6, 7, and 8 look at the issues of leadership and the social sector. In this chapter, we look at the first two points—the impact of new technologies on thought and the creation of new types of knowledge.

Digital Epistemology and Smart Technologies

Epistemology is the study of knowledge, including an understanding of its nature, its valid methodologies, the nature and conditions for its growth and application, and, ultimately, pedagogies of learning and investigation. Throughout history, knowledge and the media in which it is generated and recorded have developed in tandem. Knowledge essentially involves the use of code, or a process of encoding (in memory, on paper, by a computer). The nature of the code and the coding process used set limits and define possibilities for knowledge. Using this idea as our rubric, we offer a sketch of three stages of knowledge and media: (1) the classical period, (2) the Middle Ages to roughly the present, and (3) the postmodern period of digital information and smart technology.

In early classical times, knowledge was based (encoded) in dialogue and close proximity to the life of a master teacher. It is difficult to imagine the teachings of Socrates apart from the person Socrates, just as it may be difficult today to imagine the music of a pop star apart from that performer. Hence, knowing involved extensive performative components, and as we know from Plato's "Seventh Letter" and the pedagogies of the Academy and Lyceum (and others), the most important knowledge products of this period were understood to be produced only in live dialogue among an inner circle living in close proximity and daily conversation and debate.[2]

By the Middle Ages, the literary text and the scribe, with Scripture as the paradigm, became central to knowledge and its tasks. The central intellectual project became *"explication de text,"* the responsive reading and commentary on texts that formed a central activity of monastic life and the medieval university. With the advent of the printing press, the culture of the book expanded greatly to include a wide public. Protestantism contributed another impetus to the dynamic, with its emphasis on the examination of conscience, which led to keeping personal journals and reinforced the creation and audience for novels that explored character, such as the novels of Jane Austen. Victorian aspirations toward universal literacy provided another stimulus to literary culture and generated a vast new domain of popular penny newspapers and magazines. This text system continued to hold dominance until the end of the twentieth century, when electronic media and the Internet began to alter the landscape.

The unifying feature of this long period is the central role of the book, or text, as the medium in which knowledge is created, preserved, and transmitted. The creation, preservation, transmission, and communication channels of text-based knowledge required vast institutional structures, including extensive networks of public, private, and academic libraries, with their catalogues and systems. Within this framework, schools and universities served as the principal communication channels through which authorized, text-based knowledge and discussion flowed. Outside the academic setting, the truth-value of folkloric and popular text knowledge was more dubious and deemed to hold an inferior epistemic value. The textual basis of knowledge has held sway for such a long time that it is tempting to see textuality and knowledge as inextricable. Indeed, we hear various pundits and scholars today complain about the declining centrality of book culture as a critical decline in brainpower and knowledge. But is it?

As we understand now from cybernetics and computers, software and hardware are separate things. The same software can run on different hardware. Or put differently, hardware "underdetermines" software. The distributed hardware of book culture—texts, libraries, catalogues, disciplinary boundaries, academic channels of communication, and validation for new texts—underdetermines knowledge and its growth, just as oral culture underdetermined knowledge in its day. This underdetermination of software by hardware helps to put in perspective the famous "interdetminancy of translation" concept argued by Harvard logician W. V. Quine several decades ago. It also sheds light on Zeno's paradoxes from the ancient world. Douglas Hofstadter, in *Gödel, Escher, Bach,* also points out several occasions when higher-level orders are "underdetermined" by the lower levels—a spoken word cannot be parsed into a discrete set of phonemes without some gap. Gaps, lacunae, and holes in the fabric of the world and our knowledge are inevitable and are indicative of structural features of the hierarchic organization of data.

The issue is best understood as one of perspective. From the perspective of classical oral culture, the loss of close contact with the master teacher, who embodied a form of knowing, and the loss of extensive memorization of dialogue and ideas "learned by heart" must have seemed like the end of culture. How could the Homeric poet imagine the literary consciousness of Jane Austen's readership? It was unimaginable. Similarly, in the Middle Ages, the introduction of Arabic numbers was resisted for a time within academic circles precisely because arithmetic was so much easier to perform with Arabic numbers than with Roman numerals. Multiplication and division are very complex processes with Roman numerals, and so, it was argued, using the old medium developed greater intellectual strength and ability, as if mathematical thinking were a form of weightlifting. As we know, the reverse was the case. Ease of calculation led to a quantum growth of mathematical reasoning, and entire new forms of previously unimagined mathematics were ultimately created.

The introduction of significantly new media for use in creating, recording, and disseminating knowledge is tied to explosive intellectual growth, although it is destabilizing and destructive to the older media and its authorities. The new knowledge created in such new media takes a form that is unimaginable from within the symbol system and codes of the previous system. The master teacher's spoken word and the authorized text have been the only two media available to date for knowledge. Digitization and smart technologies represent the first major epistemological break since textuality replaced oral culture.

At this early stage, it is difficult, perhaps impossible, to imagine the changes in knowledge that will result from the introduction of new media. Some features already stand out. For one thing, new media combine text, image, sound, and dialogue in new ways that are likely to elevate the role of images and music. The dominant role of text is not assured. Authority and comparability are also distributed in the electronic medium. On the computer screen, it is possible to place a Ming vase side by side with Keats's "Ode on a Grecian Urn" or a painting by Jackson Pollack while listening to U-2 or Beethoven through the Internet. What do such juxtapositions suggest or imply? Access to primary texts and data is open, potentially, to every learner in the future. How does this decentralize authority? When the school and its authorized curriculum no longer represent the only access to knowledge, how is the role of the academy and school to be adjusted alongside the growing number of rich knowledge sources available electronically? Today, of course, much of the information on the Web is unreliable, as is much of the information stored in books. It is also true, as Mary Walshok and others point out, that the academy is no longer the only institutional base for research and the creation of new knowledge.[3] Corporate-based research and development more than rivals university research, and as a result, transmission of expertise and data across the boundaries between universities and the private sector is on the rise. Implicit in this transfer is a shift away from the academy as the central authority on knowledge.

The expanse, variety, and flexibility of the new media of digitized knowledge and smart technologies suggest a new model of knowledge that can be understood in contrast with the prevailing model of the modern period. The overriding ideal of the modern period, modeled on propositions printed in a text, was that of a complete system of knowledge. Newton's *Principia Mathematica* epitomized the ideal, perhaps seemed to have achieved it. As Alexander Pope wrote:

> Nature and Nature's Law lay hid in night.
> God said, "Let Newton be," and all was light.[4]

With time, careful thought, and accumulating evidence, thinkers in the modern period maintained that a complete system of knowledge could be created that systematically linked all possible true propositions into a single valid theory, or worldview. As envisioned, such a system would be a finite set of statements, each of which is true and can be logically derived or connected with each and every other statement in the set. If achieved, such a model of knowledge would have a static finality, every truth would be explicitly and precisely stated, and every explicit well-formed formula would have its precisely correct place in the logical tree of deductions. The ghost of this vision still lives today when string theory scientists suggest that they are close to a "theory of everything."

With the exception of Newton, successive attempts to create a text containing such a complete system of knowledge produced conflicting versions: Cartesian, Humean, Kantian, Hegelian, Carnapian, and others. The *coup d'état*, however, came with Kurt Gödel's *Incompleteness Theorem* in the early twentieth century. Gödel proved that no logical system of propositions can be both complete and true. That is, if a system is logically complete, or closed, some truths will fall necessarily outside the system. The ideal of a total logical system of knowledge is logically impossible.

Clay tablets, parchments, and printed books encode information and ideas in fixed and unchangeable media. Once the code is inscribed, it is unchanging and complete. The electronic medium is by its nature malleable, interactive, and fluid. It seems unavoidable, therefore, that the knowledge created, stored, and transmitted through this fluid medium should incorporate a dynamic quality in its essence. In contrast with the model of a finite, completable system of knowledge, which textuality suggested as the goal, electronically encoded knowledge suggests a different image—the image of a dynamic, flexible network of information that is infinitely malleable and able to be constructed in multiple ways. The old model of knowledge took structural features of the written text as structures of knowledge; for example, like texts, knowledge was supposed to proceed in linear, complete, logical sequence. Instead of a building with its foundation and linear construction and structure, electronic media suggest the structure of networks or the image of the ocean. In the old model, mastery was conceived as complete comprehension of all propositional truths: mastery of the total text. With the emerging new model, mastery must be understood more like an artist's knowledge of how to create valuable new combinations from the vast data available or a seaman's skill in knowing how to navigate across a vast, dynamic region that cannot be known in full. Knowledge becomes a work of art.

At the core of this new concept of a more dynamic knower is a focus, or inner equilibrium, that provides a counterweight to a dynamic and unbounded field. This idea of an inner governing mechanism, or compass, mirrors the idea of such a mechanism for happiness. Instead of knowing a finite and logically complete set of truths, the master knower in the digital age is dynamic and creative in response to a dynamic field of expanding knowledge and continuous learning. The governing force in such activity—an equilibrium created between the knower and the known—produces an optimal operation on both sides (Figure 3). On one side is the inner equilibrium of the knower (like a center of gravity for a gymnast); on the other side of the dynamic is a created pattern,

or order, that uses the structures of the external field to create a
new pattern dynamic (like the gymnastic routine created by using
the forces of the physical world). The focal point and the field
become linked in a dynamic interaction. Knowing, in this model,
is a creative and constructive addition to the world. Like the quality of mercy, it is twice blessed; it blesses the knower and it blesses the known. This, in turn, suggests some psychological, ecological, and commercial norms for knowledge in the digital age.

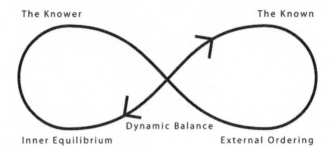

The Knower   The Known

Dynamic Balance

Inner Equilibrium   External Ordering

Figure 3 Equilibrium Between the Knower and the Known

A gymnast is able to be fluid and creative in performing a
gymnastic routine, having developed a sense of a personal center
of gravity through training. Focus on this center of gravity gives
the gymnast the ability to be off balance and to propel his/her
body through space, using the limitations of gravity as "hardware" to create the routine's "software," or design. A similar skill
will be demanded for knowledge in the future.

The implications of smart technologies for knowledge and
culture are legion. Do the dynamic flexibility and artistic
dimension of digital knowing mean that "anything goes," as
Richard Rorty suggests?[5] Hardly. Not every routine or every
gymnastic performance is equal. The new standards and criteria for dynamic, digitally based knowing are just emerging and
still carry the experimental and provisional stamp of the new.
Smart technologies learn as they process data; the marketing
software for Amazon.com is a simple example. Smart goggles

are used in advanced manufacturing to project blue-line circuit design onto a surface for one eye while the other eye sees the board that is being made into a circuit board. Smart desktops help learners access information that targets strategies for the next stages of learning and knowledge growth. These are but a few examples of what is emerging around us today.

Smart technologies extend the boundary of knowledge beyond the human mind. This is a completely new possibility. Books extended the capacity to store knowledge beyond the gray matter of the brain, but smart technologies extend the capacity to learn, to change and enhance information beyond the human mind. Distributing learning across a network of human beings and smart devices and machines is a radical shift. Smart technologies create a more permeable boundary between subject and object, between persons and the world. Again, from the perspective of past humanism and past ideologies, this is a destabilizing prospect. Humanism has been understood as an affirmation of the primacy of the human, and this tends to be extended to mean that the boundary between the human and nonhuman is inviolate. Like the conflation of knowledge with textual literacy, however, this seems to confuse medium and message.

Three striking hallmarks of digitally based knowledge stand out that are likely to affect ways to understand knowledge in the future. First, digitally based knowledge is encoded in malleable multimedia and endlessly dynamic systems. Second, it is interactive, decentralized, and potentially pervasive everywhere all the time. Third, it exists in distributed smart technologies that have the capacity to learn with us in the evolution of knowledge. Together, these structural features of digitized knowledge and smart technologies hold forth the possibility of unleashing the power of continuous learning that has been limited in the past by oral and textual systems for encoding, storing, and transmitting knowledge.

New Topology of Knowledge

Disciplinary boundaries, created by text-based systems of knowledge and university systems, are often barriers to intellec-

tual innovation in the digital age. Today, some of the most innovative work is occurring across discipline boundaries: for example, in the intersection of biology and engineering. Traditional discipline boundaries also tend to hinder a new vision of knowledge.
What were the reasons for these boundaries in the first place?

Aristotle argued that different types of being require different
ways of knowing, or different sciences, with diverse methods
and degrees of certainty. Mathematics, for example, is a science of
abstract relations, such as continuity and spatial form, and uses a
deductive method and carries with it a high degree of certainty.
Ethics, on the other hand, he argued, deals with experience and
perceptual judgment and is far less exact. Because there are multiple types of existence, it is necessary to have multiple sciences
and multiple methods, yielding different degrees of certainty and
reliable knowledge.

Starting with Descartes, scientists and philosophers in the
modern period rejected Aristotle's conception and insisted
instead that existence is singular and unified. There are not different types of being but a single continuous existence, according
to the modern view. Something either exists or does not. As a
result, modern science sought to develop a single scientific
method that would produce a single and unified account of all
that exists—the dream of a complete, unified science, already
examined. This assumption about the unity of existence explains
why "reductionism," that is, the attempt to reduce everything to
mere physical existence and causation, became the goal of modern science and the outcome feared by theologians and humanists alike. In this view, disciplinary boundaries marked the places
where reduction would occur. Nothing interesting or creative
could emerge at the boundaries of disciplines.

Today, we see many new ideas and new knowledge coming
from the overlap of disciplines. Today, new insights about the
structure, or topology, of knowledge are likely to come from
cybernetics, systems theory, and network theory. From cybernetics, we are learning about the structural characteristics of information. Our growing awareness of the pervasive presence of

information and cybernetic structure in nature is also leading to new perspectives on the nature of physical existence and how human knowledge of the physical world should be shaped. Information has an inherent hierarchical structure that separates "software" from "hardware"—the code from the markers and materials in which the code is inscribed. The string code in a computer operating system is not the material or medium in which it is written, any more than the word dignity is the marks of ink on a piece of paper.

These features would suggest now that the world is not a unitary existence but a hierarchic order built around the inherent hierarchy of code and medium. This in turn would suggest that multiple, interlacing forms of existence are the object of knowledge and so will require multiple overlapping disciplines and methods.

William Wimsatt, a biologist and philosopher at the University of Chicago, has suggested that knowledge has an irreducibly complex and dynamic structure, or topology, in which distinct domains of truth and causality exist and overlap. The boundaries between different domains are not hard and fast, as old-fashioned theories held; nor are they simply zones of incompleteness that will eventually be filled in with enough detail to erase. Instead, Wimsatt and others argue, the borders between domains are porous and interactive in ways that defy single analysis. He uses the suggestive term "causal thickets" for the boundaries. In such "causal thickets," the density and complexity of interaction create a genuine boundary. In this model of knowledge, knowledge is not a linear structure that moves from a foundation to a top level but a complex network of domains that overlap, where they do, in dynamic "thickets" of complexity.

Systems theory and hierarchy theory are also making the organizational benefits of hierarchy clear. According to studies of physical networks and lattices, a new level of organization uses the limitations of the lower-level organization to create a new range of freedom and capacity. The repeated lattice structure of molecules in a crystal creates the condition for the hexagonal surface shape of the crystal, which in turn enables new forms of organization and bonding. In general, the organizational structure of a lower order in a hierarchy creates a boundary, but that boundary creates a new range of freedom for the higher level of organization. Growing understanding of these structural features, together with the dynamic and flexible structure of digitally encoded knowledge, will provide a framework for a more flexible and dynamic topology of knowledge.

Human beings, in distinction from physical, biotic, and psychical entities, function as active agents in the entire range of fundamental modal dimensions—they think; they speak; they believe. To achieve the internal equilibrium, or focus, necessary in the digital age, these aspects of human awareness and activity need to be integrated. This is fundamentally an educative process, which requires a level of integration of study and development of understanding beyond data. We need to rethink knowledge in the digital age. Universities and humanities scholars have the opportunity to provide leadership in redesigning disciplinary boundaries and in articulating an expanded concept of knowledge that is both more open to the world and life affirming.

In a controversial work, sociologist Christopher Smith has argued that it is not odd to think that moral, believing, narrating animals—as opposed to both rational, acquisitive, exchanging animals and genetically adaptive and governed animals—would develop beliefs, symbols, and practices about the reality of an empirical order that makes claims to organize and guide human life.[6] **As moral animals, humans are inescapably interested in and guided by *normative cultural orders* that specify what is good, right, true, beautiful, worthy, noble, and just in life and what is not.** To be a human—to possess an identity, to act with agency—requires locating one's life within a larger moral order by which to know who one is and how one ought to live. Self, life, history, and the world are not self-interpreting in meaning. In order to make sense of the meaning of self, life, history, and the world, one has to get outside of them, to transcend them and interpret them within horizons and frameworks of perspective derived from beyond the object of interpretation. In Western civilization, the primary shapers of historical experience have been the religion of classical Greece and Rome, Judaism, Christianity, and after the Enlightenment, various forms of humanism. Reinhold Niebuhr emphasized the tension inherent in the paradoxical human experience of simultaneous finitude as material animals and transcendence in self-consciousness.[7] Have we moved ahead this argument, or have we lost ourselves in a deepening spiral of more information and less coherence? Do the times we half-create and half-inhabit demand more: a better theory of reality?

Perhaps we need to look more closely and develop an understanding of the multidimensional character of social reality, a polyphonic version that is all-inclusive. All institutions function in all kinds of ways in all the modes of human existence and experience. One can distinguish various dimensions of reality, but these never appear in isolation from one another. The coherence of reality means that the task of isolating any one dimension involves considerable theoretical abstraction.

Although there is a central unity of human life, reality points to a great diversity of aspects in empirical reality within which human life functions and exists. Perhaps Dutch theorist of jurisprudence Herman Dooyeweerd came closest to explaining this when he suggested that our temporal empirical horizon has various aspects: numerical; spatial; extensive movement; energy, in which we experience the physiochemical relations of empirical reality; biotic, or that of organic life; feeling and sensation; and logical, that is, the analytical manner of distinction in our temporal experience, which lies at the foundation of all our concepts and logical judgments. Then there is a historical aspect, in which we experience the cultural manner of development of our societal life, followed by the aspect of symbolical signification, lying at the foundation of all empirical linguistic phenomena. Furthermore, there is the aspect of social intercourse, with its rules of courtesy, politeness, good breeding, and fashion. This experiential mode is followed by the economic, aesthetic, juridical, and moral aspects, and, finally, the aspect of faith, or belief.[8]

Here, the humanities have much to add, since they are all-encompassing and not the domain of any single scientific discipline or mode of inquiry. In a recent essay, Vartan Gregorian argued that a major failure of our higher education/humanities system is that it has come to serve as a job-readiness program. "In fact mass education and the public humanities are heading toward the Home Depot approach to education, where there is no differentiation between consumption and digestion, and no guidance—or even questioning—about what it means to be an educated and cultured person."[9] This could be because we have no agreed vision of reality as much as the tenor of these times, which too often stress the practical over the intellectual faculties.

"Where is the wisdom we have lost in knowledge?" T. S. Eliot once asked. "Where is the knowledge we have lost in information?" The public humanities and our universities must once again play a critical role in rediscovering that knowledge and that wisdom, or they will become what Eliot described in a commentary on Dante's *Inferno*, where hell is a place where nothing connects with nothing. The need is for a theory of reality that is both coherent and not reductionistic. We all clamor about the fact that knowledge has been fragmented, disjointed into atomized disciplines and subdisciplines and into smaller and smaller unconnected fragments of academic specialization. What the world needs now, however, is help in integrating and synthesizing into a more comprehensive whole the exponential increases brought about by technological advances and specialization. To quote Gregorian, "Understanding the nature of knowledge and its uses, its varieties, its limitations, and abuses, is necessary for the success of our democracy." The stakes are high. Greater fragmentation, loss of richness, and conversations with smaller and smaller subdisciplinarians lead to a kind of myopia. Can the humanities, as the lifelong learning societies they were originally conceived to be, provide an antidote to glue together again all the many pieces?

Notes

1. Thomas Kuhn, *The Structure of Scientific Revolutions,* 3rd ed. (Chicago: University of Chicago Press, 1996).
2. Pierre Hadot, *What Is Ancient Philosophy* (Cambridge, MA: Harvard University Press, Belknap Press, 2004).
3. Mary Walshok, *Knowledge Without Borders: What American Research Universities Can Do for the Economy, Workplace and the Community* (Hoboken, NJ: Jossey-Bass, 1995).
4. A. Williams, ed., *Poetry and Prose of Alexander Pope* (Boston, MA: Houghton Mifflin, 1969).
5. Richard Rorty, *Philosophy and the Mirror of Nature* (Princeton, NJ: Princeton University Press, 1981).
6. Christopher Smith, *Moral, Believing Animals: Human Personhood and Culture* (Oxford: Oxford University Press, 2003).
7. Reinhold Niebuhr, *The Nature and Destiny of Man: A Christian Interpretation* (Louisville, KY: Westminster John Knox Press, 1996), pp. 13–14.
8. Herman Dooyeweerd, *A New Critique of Theoretical Thought,* rev. ed. (Philadelphia: Mellen Press, 1997).
9. Vartan Gregorian, *Chronicle of Higher Education* 50 (June 4, 2004): 39.

6

Leading, Learning, and Living as Works of Art

A

T THIS POINT, it may be helpful to take our bearings by
surveying the line of thinking over the past few chapters
and then to scan the horizon ahead. In Chapter 4, our
brief history of the humanities revealed how the liberal arts and
the humanities moved away from their original purpose—to provide a foundation and education for democratic leadership and
to support human flourishing—to become focused on marginal
counternarratives to the "pursuit of happiness." This has created
a divide between culture and the forces of commerce, technology,
and science; that divide, in turn, creates great risks for advances
in these areas in times of global change. In Chapter 5, we identified four key areas of change in which the humanities are needed to play a constructive role in developing bold new ideas to
undergird advances in other areas:

1. a new theory of knowledge (epistemology) suitable to
    new media and smart technologies;

2. a new topology of knowledge that goes beyond discipline
    barriers and old-fashioned "reductive materialism";

3. new models for leadership for open networks of innova-
    tion and entrepreneurship;

4. a positive definition of the so-called nonprofit sector and new understandings of how the government, corporate, and nonprofit sectors work together in a global knowledge-based society/economy to advance human happiness and well-being.

In addition, the humanities have a critical role to play in interpreting the "pursuit of happiness," developing understanding of the concept of "spiritual capital" outlined in Chapter 2, and helping to create new understandings of the "transcendent" sources of knowledge and action.

As we saw in the previous chapter, our understanding of knowledge and its structure is being changed by the new media and smart technologies that are now being created to store, connect, and transmit knowledge. Major changes of media—from oral tradition and dialogue to the written word and books and today from books to digital media and smart technologies—actually increase the capacity for new knowledge and new forms of learning.

The nature, roles, and scope of leadership and culture are also expanding, like our horizon for knowledge. In this chapter, we begin to outline some new ways of thinking about leadership, looking at leadership *as a work of art*. Chapter 7 looks at leadership in global, community, and organizational contexts.

Today, leaders are called on to develop skills that are like those of an artist. Like artists, leaders have to select key elements out of a vast amount of data, discern where human interests and values tend, and create something new that attracts the interest and support of others. Like a master artist, leaders today lead by creating value.

In order to understand this better, it is also important to understand something about art. For too long, we have thought of art as a form of emotion or ornament, as something nice but not necessary and certainly not strategic or a form of strategic knowledge.

However, in the current knowledge and innovation-driven world, it is not too much to say that art is a form of knowing that necessarily holds a new, higher status and function in major areas of life. Today, leading, learning, and living need to be anchored in art as a (1) symbolic system of knowledge, (2) model for creativity and innovation, and (3) basic strategy and skill for learning and judgment. Like the famous cornerstone that the builders of Solomon's temple threw away on the rubbish heap, art, reconceived and understood in today's context, may be a cornerstone to effective, prosperous, and humane judgment.

The arts and humanities manifest significant structure, which is often neglected in favor of so-called affective qualities. The arts are a powerful symbol system, like that of number and language; they are multisensory and engage multiple forms of intelligence; they employ distinctive, nonlinear forms of thinking and problem solving; and they create some of our most powerful forms of symbolic communication. Indeed, new understandings of knowing and learning and even new economic trends are coming together to support the idea that the arts are a fundamental model of knowing and learning. Far from being peripheral to the basic business of learning and knowing in school, the laboratory, society, and the corporate sector, the arts embody processes of thinking and learning that are central to the new types of "knowers" needed for the emerging "knowledge society." Viewed from this vantage point, the arts may not only join other subjects in the "core" curriculum but also take a central place. Because coming to recognize the strong cognitive dimensions of art as a way of knowing is central to understanding a new role for art, we examine a new role for art in the learning process before turning to look at the emerging importance of art as a central model of leadership and living.

In the rest of this chapter, we examine, first, some ways to begin to understand art as a form of knowledge and how this affects our understanding of learning. This has implications for how leaders are educated and the role of the arts in this process. Second, we examine five views on what works of art really are: subjective constructs or real things added to the world. These five views are also applicable to how we think about other intellectual constructs, or "intellectual property." Theoretic models in sci-ence (like the model of the gene or a new drug), social models, and mathematical formulas are like works of art in that they are created by human minds. Increasingly, these creations are of great economic value—again, like works of art. Leaders today need to understand these issues, as philosophical and arcane as they appear on the surface, as we wrestle with the role of knowl-edge products, ownership questions, purposes of research, and other issues. Finally, we examine a model of personal leadership that highlights the qualities of leadership in the context of turbu-lence and change—unavoidable qualities of today's world. This model of leadership brings us back to the model of the master artist who is able to make decisive, creative choices in the context of many uncontrollable and unpredictable forces and whose cre-ations take on a life of their own. These, too, are qualities demanded of today's leaders.

Learning as a Work of Art

Economic changes are perhaps the most obvious factors reshaping education today. It is now a commonplace to note that American schools are still organized on an industrial model developed in the last century to prepare people to work in the industrial economy. A new economic order is now emerging, however, and this economic order is based on information and knowledge, not on materials and manufacturing. Aware of this, American corporations and private-sector leaders have taken a leading role in insisting on restructuring schools to adapt them to the needs of the emerging "knowledge" economy and socie-ty.

In *The Work of Nations*, Robert Reich argues that whatever one's job title may be, only three job functions are economically meaningful now: routine production workers, in-person service providers, and what he calls "symbol analysts."[1] Symbol analysts are the new workers of the knowledge economy and create value through the analysis of symbols (information), the addition of design, and the creation of new ideas. According to Reich, the work of the symbol analyst is the engine driving the new, emerging global economy.

The kinds of skills needed by symbol analysts are quite different from the skills needed by the workers and managers of the industrial era. The "new basics" being demanded by the new economy are skills that are centered in design, communication, and learning. Walter Wriston, financial innovator and former CEO of Citibank, has written that "information is the new raw material of wealth and opportunity . . . sorting out opportunities from an overwhelming flow of information is now the prime responsibility of any good management."[2] In other words, the ability to learn and to discern patterns, interest points, and other qualities of creative design are key skills for the information age.

From this brief sketch, we see that economic forces connected with the emerging knowledge society are creating a need for a "new basics" for schools. These new basics are not simply higher-order thinking skills but rather different-order thinking skills. These skills relate to communication and design—to creating value through the creation of meaning—and this is at the heart of the creative process of the arts. Also fundamental in this new economic order is the ability to continue to learn: to love learning. Again, the creative process is a basic model for continuous, highly motivated perpetual learning.

Reflecting on learning carries us into the next area to look at new understandings about the nature of knowledge. For at least the past four hundred years in the West, we have entertained the view that knowledge is stable, sequential, provable, and finite. Sir Isaiah Berlin gave a succinct statement of this viewpoint in *The Crooked Timber of Humanity,* writing that we have believed that "a) to all genuine questions there is one true answer and one only; b) that the true answers to such questions are in principle knowable; and c) that these true answers cannot clash with each other . . . according to some they form a logical system each ingredient of which logically entails and is entailed by all the other elements."[3] This view of knowledge has provided the framework for thinking about schools and curriculum.

Contrast with this view our new understandings of knowledge as a dynamic, changing system. Instead of speaking of "knowledge," in fact, it might be better to speak of "knowing." This emphasizes the ongoing activity involved: a type of pursuit. Instead of seeing knowledge as a sequentially constructed building based on a foundation of "basic" truth and knowledge, we are now realizing that knowledge is a dynamic and ever-expanding field. The process of knowing, likewise, is not a passive storage of information and skill but instead an active, creative process. Even in math and science—the old bastions of stable, building-block knowledge—we find evidence of continuous rethinking, redrawing of conceptual lines, and creative large-scale revisions of the type described by Thomas Kuhn in *The Structure of Scientific Revolutions.*

In other areas, cognitive psychology is revealing to us more about the role of the mind in the active construction of knowledge and experience. We are just beginning to understand how dynamic the relation between the knower and the known truly is. Information theory and complexity theory are also adding to the picture with powerful new tools for understanding systems that are not simple, linear systems. Learning and knowing are themselves examples of complex, nonlinear systems, and we are just beginning to have the conceptual tools to understand them appropriately.

The educational bottom line to all these new understandings about the nature of knowing is that the old academic categories about subjects and curriculum construction no longer make sense. The student of today faces a vast universe of knowledge that is not only larger in scale than that of the past but also in a state of dynamic change. Knowledge is growing exponentially, theories are continuously reshaped, and cultures and disciplines are intersecting and interacting in new and unpredictable ways. It no longer makes practical sense—nor is it intellectually sound—to approach the curriculum as we have in the past.

Some of the most exciting work going on in the academy today is in the so-called hyphenated disciplines—bioengineering and psycholinguistics and the like—in what Michael Polanyi calls the "overlapping academic neighborhoods." Ernest Boyer has observed that

> the truth is that the old academic boxes do not fit the new intellectual questions. . . . during the coming decades, we will see a fundamental reshaping of the typology of knowledge as profound as that which occurred in the nineteenth century. . . . And wouldn't it be tragic if a nineteenth-century curriculum design continued to be imposed on schools at the very time scholars were redefining the structure of knowledge for the twenty-first century? . . . Wouldn't it be exciting . . . if we would start to rethink the nature of the new knowledge . . . ? How can we organize knowledge in a way that seems to make it relevant and powerful for students in the days ahead? Wouldn't it be exciting if both kindergarten teachers and college professors could view knowledge using understandable categories that would be newly integrated and would spiral upward in common discourse?[4]

This reshaping of the "typology of knowledge" that Boyer speaks of will include the arts, which will be repositioned in the new intellectual landscape. The opportunity now exists for the arts to reexamine themselves as a form of thinking and knowing and to assume a central intellectual role in schools of the knowledge society. The arts as a creative process provide a unique standpoint for the construction of a new curriculum that addresses the new "basics" of the knowledge society and is true to the "new typology of knowledge" to which Boyer refers.

One could add to Boyer's list of tantalizing questions. Wouldn't it be exciting to include creative artists in the process of reshaping schools? Wouldn't it be exciting to design ways to incorporate the arts and the creative process of art making into new, nonsequential curricula that are created proactively by teachers and students? Wouldn't it be exciting to rethink the nature of learning so that the creative, constructive process that we now see to be the basis of knowing would become dominant in the teaching and learning process in schools? Wouldn't it be exciting to shift our focus in schools from "knowledge transmission and storage" to "knowledge understanding and creation," from "knowledge acquisition" to "knowledge generation and creation"?

We pointed out earlier that human beings distinctively are free to choose how we interpret experience. The human predicament is characterized by the ordeal of having to continually create ourselves and our understanding of the world, based on our experience of it. This task is accomplished through learning. Our *imagination* and our intelligence are the faculties used in defining ourselves as individuals and in giving meaning to our experience of the world we inhabit; this engagement is called *learning* and is the source of our humanity. *Liberal learning* is the unique ordering of our experience in imagination; it is what makes us unique individuals. One of the most important ways in which we learn to utilize our imagination is in reconstructing the thought of another person. Through this process, we subsequently learn to find our own voice. There is a significant difference between art and entertainment. Entertainment is user oriented, or audience oriented. Art is creator oriented; that is, it calls upon us to retrace the creative process. As such, art encourages people to respond, participate, and make up their own mind; this creative inspiration to the audience encourages individuality, self-identity, and therefore freedom to define oneself. As such, art helps to promote a free society. It is this aspect of art that has been frequently lost in traditional arts education, which has too often succumbed to treating the work of art simply as a symbol for something else, or a datum, or merely decorative.

Looking at knowing as a creative, constructive process leads us to consider how the arts themselves may be viewed as a form of knowing. Of course, the arts may be approached validly from many different perspectives. On the one hand, the arts may be viewed as a formal discipline, or training, to be given to develop individual, specialized talents. Programs that give a primary value to performance skills focus on this approach. In addition, the arts may be viewed as historical artifacts that figure in a special history, namely, the history of art; they may be viewed from the point of view of the many forms of arts criticism, as the data for critical analysis as works of art; and they may be viewed as data and examples for the many theories of aesthetics that have been developed over the centuries.

On the other hand, the arts may be viewed as a symbol system, like those of language and number, created as a mode of knowing. Number systems have been created to help us describe certain features of the world that are invisible without numbers. Language is another symbol system that has been created to help us delineate features of experience and the world. Artistic symbols are yet another symbol system—nonverbal and nonmathematical—that demarcate otherwise invisible features of the world and our experience. Symbols act like the contour lines of the map maker to delineate features of the world. Symbols stabilize, fix, and give direction and meaning to experience. A subject comes to know through the act of creating and manipulating symbols in the mapping of experience. From this perspective, the arts are a major symbol system and a basic form of knowing. A work of art represents an artist's attempt to map some experience in forms that capture the essence of the experience and communicate it to others. The artistic process, then, is seen as a continuous process of noticing, symbolization, reattending, and revision. These are now central cognitive activities and features of the type of learning that leads not simply to retention of information but also to innovation.

Five Views of What Art Is

Speaking of the people represented in Rembrandt's powerful portraits, Michael Kimmelman of the *New York Times* asks, "Have you ever met anyone so authentic and remarkable?"[5] George Steiner elaborates on this notion at some length in his masterwork *Grammars of Creation*.

This is a provocative issue. Why is a representation of something in a work of art or a theory more powerful than the real thing? And what does it mean to say that it is "more powerful"? Why is Hamlet a more unforgettable person than most of the people we meet in everyday life? Is it intellectual snobbery to think this is so, or is the representative power of art somehow an additive component to reality? If it is, does this mean that, on a spectrum of reality, with the lower range moving toward the absolute zero of "nothingness," or nonexistence, and the opposite end of the spectrum populated with the genuine articles of existence (rocks, plants, animals, people, etc.), do works of art go off the top of the scale as a form of suprareality?

At one level, works of art are not real. A painting of a bowl of fruit is not a bowl of fruit. Likewise, works of art are not true. Works of art are called *fictions*, not lies or untruths, but fictions. The paradox emerges here, too, as Wallace Stevens, a master on this theme, knew, saying to the high-toned Christian woman of his poem's title—"poetry is the supreme fiction, madam."[6] As in the spectrum of reality, so on the scale of truth, with the lower end trailing toward falsehood and the upper end toward the set of all truths, art would seem to go off the scale.

There are other facets to this puzzle as well. A work of art achieves its power by a process of elimination and reduction. That is, the work of art is created by reducing the amount of data from what it "represents." Why do the depletion of information, the loss of data, and the replacement of a real thing with a representation produce more rather than less? The power achieved by Rembrandt's paintings is largely a matter of less—the use of a few dots of yellow paint to present a gold chain. The economy of characterization achieved by a great playwright or novelist illustrates the same process of elimination. Martha Graham used to say that any action done with intention is a ritual, and the power of her choreography comes by means of an intentional simplification of motion that carries the force of ritual. In a sense, art, like theory, can be defined as a method of simplification, the act of reducing the cacophony of noise to music, the jumble of bodily movement to choreography, of visual overload into painting, the buzz of daily life and history to the crisp delineation of drama. The power of elegance and elimination is also known in the sciences and mathematics. Theoretical advances are driven by simplification of data, and a mathematical solution is an elegant elision of data about the world reduced to pure symbolic relations.

This may seem counterintuitive. Take a real individual, for example. The real person is an enormously complex thing—from the vast complexity of personality, personal history, motivation, knowledge, choice, desire, complex relations with others—and all this on top of even more biological, genetic, chemical, and physical complexity. The real person is dense with layer upon layer of complexity. The ontological density of the real, existing individual would suggest that we would always experience things in the world as more real than works of art or science, which vastly simplify and leave out considerable detail and complexities.

Why is less more? Several possible answers can be suggested. First, it might be argued that real things are too dense for us to take in. Reality overloads our capacity to process it, so simplifications of reality in works of art, theories, or formulas allow our limited brains to grasp some important features. Compared with the data overload, the simplified representation has a comparatively greater impact. Second, it might be argued that by simplification, we impose or invent a human frame through which we can relate to the data. Things become "meaningful" when some type of human touch is applied to them. So by representing something in a work of art, a theory, or a mathematical formula, we are not simply eliminating excess data that we cannot process but rather are adding to the data a human perspective that tells us what matters—to us—about the object.

Third, it could be argued that the simplification of art and theory uncovers, or discovers, an "underlying structure" that is more fundamental than the whole array of data. By more fundamental, we mean that (1) the underlying structure exists in a primary way, whereas the other realities are secondary, or dependent, and (2) at the representation of this underlying structure is epistemologically primary. The relations of primary and dependent realities and truths also may indicate a causal relation of some type.

Fourth, it could be argued that the simplification does not uncover or discover something that already exists but no one had seen before, such as Mt. Everest, but instead creates something new that has a greater power, reality, and truth than the real object. Again, Wallace Stevens puts the point well in the title of one of his later poems: "Reality Is an Activity of the Most August Imagination." This view sounds like romanticism, and it does have some connections there but goes beyond it. Some mathematicians working on the most creative frontiers of higher mathematics report a sense of someone or something working along with them, as though the symbols on the page were themselves alive and impelled to do things themselves or that some other problem solver, like a chess opponent or a collaborator, was prompting solutions or forcing one to take new strategies.

Writers and artists report similar experiences when characters in their books take on a life of their own and take the authors down paths they had not intended or when the paint on the canvass redirects and inspires the emerging painting in unexpected ways. Thus, the elegantly simplified representation achieved by art and theory is a creation that exists alongside the rest of existence—the equation, the painting, the theory do exist, after all—and exists as a new, and higher, level of existence. They do go off the chart into a realm of suprareality that is both an addition to the set of existing things and an extension of the scale. A Picasso masterwork, the Beethoven *Hammerklavier* sonata, a late Bartok string quartet—all are, like Gödel's *Incompleteness Theorem* or $E = mc^2$, real entities that have come into existence through an act of creation, like a new plant or species. They add to the world's inventory of existence, and they add entities of a higher order. That is why they are more powerful than what is represented by them.

Finally, it can be argued that works of art, theory, and mathematics are powerful because they are conduits, passages, or openings to a greater power. In this view, the works themselves may or may not possess a higher level of reality, but they do point beyond themselves or open up another, higher level of reality. There are several ways to describe how this happens—to say that they "point to" or provide a passage to a higher reality describes the semantic role of the works as pointers, like a road sign, or Wittgenstein's ladder, that are important because of what they point or lead to. In this sense, they are instruments, or means, to an end, in themselves having little value. To describe artistic/theoretical works as "opening" to a higher reality implies that artistic and theoretical works have a power in themselves to open something otherwise closed. Heidegger, through what he famously called "clearings," or openings in being, used this description as a key to understanding how human beings are grounded in existence. Ultimately, such a power is valued for its transparency: its ability to allow the mind to see through and into the higher level and to be personally transformed through such insight. Transparency and transformation are inseparable in this equation; they are two sides of the same coin. As noted earlier, Rilke observed that it is impossible to see a Greek torso without hearing the command: "change thyself!" So on this account, great art and theory might be described as a power of transforming transparency and focus.

Understood as semantic pointers, or as powers to open, art and theory are seen essentially as instrumental or spiritually "therapeutic" in some ultimate way. On the other hand, if art and theory are regarded as having some substantive reality of their own under the category of transcendence, they must be understood as an "incarnation" of the higher level into the lower level of reality. That is, artworks or theories are powerful because they embody transcendence. On this elevated reading, art and theory are angelic, messengers of the divine. Rainer Maria Rilke's spectacular description of angels in "The Second Elegy" comes to mind as a description that would apply both to angels and to art and theory as incarnations of transcendence:

> ... Creation's pampered favorites,
> mountain-ranges, peaks growing red in the dawn
> of all beginning,—pollen of the flowering godhead,
> joints of pure light, corridors, stairways, thrones,
> space formed from essence, shields made of ecstasy,
> storms of emotion whirled into rapture, and suddenly,
>   alone:

    mirrors, which scoop up the beauty that has streamed
        from their face
  and gather it back, into themselves, entire.[7]

George Steiner has described a similar understanding in a more grounded context of reading and aesthetic experience. Steiner's description is anchored in the idea that in the greatest art, the symbol and the symbolized become one. In perhaps one of the most remarkable passages anywhere in literature to describe the fusion of symbol and symbolized, Steiner writes the following:

> Where we read truly, where the experience is to be that of meaning, we do so as if the text (the piece of music, the work of art) incarnates (the notion is grounded in the sacramental) a real presence of significant being. This real presence, as in an icon, as in the enacted metaphor [sic] of the sacramental bread and wine, is, finally, irreducible to any other formal articulation, to any analytic deconstruction or paraphrase. It is a singularity in which concept and form constitute a tautology, coincide point to point, energy to energy, in that excess of significance over all discreet elements and codes of meaning which we call the symbol or the agency of transparence.
>
> These are not occult notions. They are of the immensity of the commonplace. They are perfectly pragmatic, experiential, repetitive, each and every time a melody comes to inhabit us, to possess us even unbidden each and every time a poem, a passage of prose seizes upon our thought and feelings, enters into the sinews of our remembrance and sense of the future, each and every time a painting transmutes the landscapes of our previous perceptions (poplars are on fire after Van Gogh, viaducts walk after Klee). To be 'indwelt' by music, art, literature, to be made responsible, answerable to such habitation as a host is to a guest—perhaps unknown, unexpected—at evening, is to experience the commonplace mystery of a real presence. Not many of us feel compelled to, have the expressive means to, register the mastering quality of this experience—as does Proust when he crystallizes the sense of the world and of the word in the little yellow spot which is the real presence of a riverside door in Vermeer's View of Delft, or as does Thomas Mann when he enacts in word and metaphor the coming over us, the 'overcoming of us', in Beethoven's Opus 111. No matter.

> The experience itself is one we are thoroughly at home with—
> an informing idiom—each and every time we live a text, a
> sonata, a painting.[8]

Steiner's passage effectively exemplifies, or rather incarnates, the idea he is presenting. This is an unmatched passage of transparence. The unfolding thought moves from the experience of reading to the experience of achieved meaning to the concept of incarnation, sacrament, real presence, significant being, singularity, tautology, the perfect coincidence of concept and form that defies any other deconstruction or statement and comes to rest with "symbol" defined as "excess significance or agency of transparence." This lofty metaphysical riff is then said to be simple, common experience, something that happens on a daily basis whenever we are inhabited by a work of art. Experience of this sort is not an occult notion or flight of fancy, Steiner affirms, but a "commonplace mystery," a matter of being at home, that is, being most fully ourselves, most fully human, and at our ease.

Today, these five understandings of the significance of art, theory, and mathematics enter into discussion in confused, partial, and jumbled mixtures. This often produces disagreements because of the resulting confusion and equivocations. Disputes are also aggravated by either-or approaches to complex issues, like this one. The worlds of art, philosophy, science, and mathematics are so large and complex themselves that each of these understandings is needed to cover the range of issues and experiences. Why should we attempt to destroy all other points of view in favor of one alone? A broader humanism accommodates the full spectrum of understandings.

The five accounts of the power of art, theory, and numbers do seem to form a spectrum of views and responses that correspond to different levels of personal development, adventure versus anxiety, and differentiation. The first two explanations, for example, are relatively simple ideas based on deficiencies—the inability to process all the information around us and the inability to take information in without some human frame of reference. In both of these views, the power of art and theory is grounded in a human deficiency, need, and subjectivity.

The third, fourth, and fifth approaches, on the other hand, are increasingly differentiated, objective, and affirmative about art and theory. That is, they delineate the power of art and theory in what is taken to be objectively real "underlying structures," new entities of a new type in the world, and, most differentiated of all, incarnate transcendent objects.

This analysis would suggest that the first two understandings of art and theory would be attractive to those who are less likely to have a clearly defined identity, to be more anxious, to be uncomfortable with differentiation, to prefer empathy over responsibility, and to prefer social or group identity over individual identity. Thinkers who have very strong personal identities and personal autonomy, on the other hand, are more likely to understand the creations of art, theory, and mathematics in highly differentiated ways. Just as a strong leader helps an organization or a group to mature toward higher social differentiation, to take greater risks, and to stake out clear goals, so the stronger intellectual leaders will tend to objectify and differentiate the creations of art and theory.

Ironically, instead of being primitive and anthropomorphic, affirmations of artistic and theoretical reality display greater sophistication, maturity, and leadership. Instead of remaining with subjectivity and the emotional comfort of groups, powerful artists and thinkers delineate themselves sharply from what they come to know. The more powerful creators separate their own psyches and subjective experiences and feelings from the artistic and theoretical objects of their work, thereby necessarily creating or discovering a separate realm of existence inhabited by the objects of their thoughts. This greater intellectual delineation shifts the focus from the subject to the object and acknowledges a power outside the subjective experience of the creator. Put another way, weaker thinkers see their creations as parts of their own subjective experience and imagination. The creator and the creation remain in an infantile union and "empathy," often called self-expression. The more powerful thinkers clearly identify and articulate where their own powers and responsibilities begin and end and where other forces and entities come into play. This capacity for self-delineation and objectification is a sign of mastery and a sign of a self-regulating intellectual capacity that creates autonomy. **Just as leadership, liberty, and happiness all depend on a well-developed self-regulating system of character, so creative intellectual and artistic work also require self-delineation and regulation.**

Leading and Living as Works of Art

We all know some general things about leadership. Leadership consists in the ability to, first, frame a vision and, second, persuade others to work toward that goal. The ability to create a holistic vision and to harness the disparate personal agendas of others into the pursuit of that vision bears obvious analogies to the creation of a work of art. But how, precisely, do we persuade others? What does it take? One way of answering this is to say that others are persuaded to follow only by those whom they perceive as manifesting a special kind of integrity. In a world of dynamic change and innovation, leadership is a force of creativity. This requires not only a different focus for leadership, as Jerry Mechling of the Kennedy Center at Harvard University has argued, but also a more mature model of leadership. According to Edwin H. Friedman, leadership is a form of personal self-regulation that operates undisturbed through turbulence and change and manifests the following qualities:

People exercising personal leadership are marked by:

- Their relative lack of anxiety when others are anxious

- Their ability to say "I" when others are demanding they say "we"

- Their capacity to take a stand in an intense emotional situation

- Their ability to avoid being pigeonholed, stereotyped, or otherwise forced into a box that involves polarization

- Their ability to clearly identify and articulate where their own responsibilities begin and end and where others' responsibilities begin and end

- Their ability to avoid automatically being just another emotional domino in an organization or group

- Their ability to be clear about their own personal values and goals

- The fact that they take maximum responsibility for their own emotional being and destiny as opposed to blaming others or blaming the context.[9]

The classic portrait of dynamic leadership that mirrors the model Friedman describes comes from Aristotle. According to both Platonic and Aristotelian views, leadership is a quality of character rooted in judgment and a strong form of aesthetic perception. A leader is first and foremost a person who is self-governing—autonomous. *Auto-nomos*—the Greek term—is a lesson itself. The term indicates a power that flows out of the self and back into the self (*auto*) in a sustained and elegant balance. *Nomos* is the Greek for law, rule, and governance and also implies orderliness and hence beauty. Thus, the autonomous person is one from whom laws and rules flow out of the self and back into the self in a way that produces order, beauty, and self-sufficiency, self-governance, or independence. The highest end of leadership, hence, is the ability to lead one's own life. From this perspective, leadership of others is not highly desirable. In the *Republic,* Plato goes so far as to state that only those who do not want to rule in society should be permitted to rule. By that he means that only those who are autonomous, or self-governed, have the capacity for real leadership, and these individuals have the integrity to lead their own lives and prefer to do so. Civic leadership, thus, becomes an act of self-sacrifice and service to others.

Also central to this model is a form of moral judgment grounded in perception, not simply abstract theory or rules. Virtuous action and judgment are tied closely to issues that must be experienced and perceived. Generalizing from these concrete actions to rules necessarily eliminates significant data and robs the action of its informing excellence. Hence, in this view, biographies of people who demonstrate fine action, stories, literature, and other narratives that embed action in detailed situations carry the substance of moral awareness and reflection.

Like a fine artist, those who lead lives of excellence have sharply defined and nuanced perception for what Aristotle called the "Golden Mean." Often misunderstood as a thoughtless acceptance of whatever happens to be middle of the road, the Golden Mean is a rubric for a finely developed and sophisticated perception and judgment of action. Everyone has had some experience of this quality—an experience of someone who has said precisely the right thing at the right time to the right person in the right way and for the right reason. Such moments of grace, like the grace of a fine athlete, can take the breath away. They appear self-warranting, self-authorizing, and perfect—nothing could be added or taken away without loss.

More than ever, leadership in today's world is defined by these qualities, even if exemplified less often than needed. In a world in which flexible teams from different professional backgrounds, cultures, and sectors must be able to convene and work together to solve problems that cut across each of their areas of expertise and knowledge, qualities of character are more and more critical. The highest levels of ethical behavior, trust, reliability, openness, and willingness to put a higher good above the personal are needed for such flexible and changeable teams to function. Without individuals of such character, teams collapse, and the impact on the society outside the team is greater today than ever.

The challenges facing civic leaders today also require self-governance and a desire to serve rather than to dominate. As books like *The Only Sustainable Advantage* point out, people and communities are now critical drivers of economic growth. Hence, competitive economic strategy, a core concern of civic leaders, is today grounded in a new form of civic dialogue. Civic leaders today find it necessary to build connections, shared understanding, and consensus across dispersed networks that harness brainpower, innovation, and culture. Effective strategy can no longer come from a small group of business or government leaders acting alone or only within their own sectors. This requires an autonomous form of leadership that exhibits the maturity described by Friedman and the integrity of character and judgment described by Aristotle. Leadership is more like the action of an artist, one that serves the greater good.

Applying the model of artistry to life, Montaigne wrote: "to compose our character is our duty, not to compose books, and to win, not battles and provinces, but order and tranquility in our conduct. Our great and glorious masterpiece is to live appropriately."[10] Or as Thoreau put it in *Walden*, "it is something to be able to paint a particular picture, or to carve a statue, and so to make a few objects beautiful; but it is far more glorious to carve and paint the very atmosphere and medium through which we look, which morally we can do. To affect the quality of the day, that is the highest of arts."[11] Such is the artistry of life and leadership.

Notes

1. Robert Reich, *The Work of Nations: Preparing Ourselves for 21st Century Capitalism* (New York: Random House, 1992).
2. Walter Wriston, *The Twilight of Sovereignty* (New York: Replica Books, 1997).
3. Isaiah Berlin, *The Crooked Timber of Humanity* (New York: Alfred A. Knopf, 1991), p. 209.
4. Ernest Boyer, *On Common Ground* (New Haven, CT: Yale University Press, 1994), p. 11.
5. Michael Kimmelman, "Humanities with Flaws Forgiven," *New York Times*, January 28, 2005.
6. Wallace Stevens, "A High-Toned Old Christian Woman," *Poems* (New York: Vintage Books, 1959), p. 26.
7. Rainer Maria Rilke, "The Second Elegy," *The Selected Poetry of Rainer Maria Rilke*, ed. and trans. by Stephen Mitchell (New York:

Vintage International Books, 1989), p. 157.

8. George Steiner. *No Passion Spent* (New Haven, CT: Yale University Press, 1998), p. 35.

9. Edwin H. Friedman, *Reinventing Leadership: Change in an Age of Anxiety Discussion Guide* (New York: Guildford Press, 1996), p. 11.

10. Michel Montaigne, *Essays,* in Harold Bloom, *The Western Canon* (New York: Penguin Putnam, 1994), p. 156.

11. Henry Thoreau, *Walden: Or Life in the Woods* (New York: Dover, 1995), p. 79.

7

Leadership in a Global Society

Globalization and Localization

THE WORLD WE KNEW is now completely transformed. **The new integrated knowledge economy of global proportions is free from the confines and shackles of the past. That world is becoming more and more boundaryless.** And its emerging shape will dictate the course of this new century. Global organizations themselves are now the agents of massive international economic change.

The phenomenon of globalization details a large and growing contribution of international corporations to national economies. Globalization involves the flow of investments, goods, services, people, technologies, culture, and ideas across borders. On the surface, the facts bear out the process. Foreign firms now account for a growing share of production and employment in almost every developed country. Foreign firms produced a greater percentage of manufacturing output in the United States, accounting for a tenth of jobs in manufacturing. Britain, Canada, and Sweden display a similar trend. According to UN data, an astonishing 66% of output and 47% of employment in Ireland come from foreign firms. These firms are not as dominant every-where—Germany and France, for example—and in Japan, for-eign firms scarcely figure; they employ a mere 0.8% of workers.

Globalization and interdependence are growing in impor-tance for four reasons.

1. Foreign firms pay their workers more than the national average, and the gap is widening.

2. Foreign firms create jobs more quickly than their domes-tic counterparts do. In the United States, again, the work-force of foreign firms rose from 1989 to 2001 compared with domestic ones.

3. Foreign firms spend more heavily on research and devel-opment in the countries where they invest: in 2004, 15% of U.S. R&D, 20% of France's, and a remarkable 40% of Britain's.

4. Foreign firms tend to export more than domestic firms do. In 2004 in Ireland, for instance, they exported some 90% of their output. The gap was similar in the Netherlands; an exception here is the United States.

The benefits of trade and investment are clear, and the trend is moving in one direction. Globalization is apparently here to stay; like modernization or secularization, it is a general phenom-enon progressing at a rapid pace, and it is no longer possible to put the genie back into its bottle.

Today, global organizations are the important actors, and they succeed to the degree that they comprehend the demands of this new and highly competitive environment. All individuals—and even governmental and not-for-profit entities—would bene-fit greatly from following in the footsteps or in the wake of these awesome yet nimble global corporations. Arguably, globalization faces these giant players first, and their reaction to the processes of acting in a globally integrated fashion in turn affects everyone else. Their reactions to the processes of globalization over the previous decade, and into the future, are critical to understand-ing which forces, ideas, and worldviews are most likely to shape our shared future, to form our civilization. Globalization may have its discontents, but it is a proverbial giant let loose and simply cannot be wished away. Its benefits are legion, and like other processes of creative destruction, its negative effects will be either ameliorated or short-lived.

Localization

As global dynamics in economics, knowledge, and culture become increasingly powerful, a complementary power develops for localities that understand their role in the global order. Ironically, globalization results in an enhanced value for the local: localization. As economist Michael Porter of Harvard's Center for Economic Competitiveness points out, when most sources of economic competitiveness are equalized by globalization, the only nonfungible source of competitive advantage is the local community and its human assets.[1] Or, to be more precise, the knowledge, sophistication, demands, and culture of a local population and community become critical sources of competitive advantage in a global setting.

Here again, humanities organizations and programs can play an important, creative role if they choose to do so. Public humanities programs can be designed intentionally to enhance and amplify local assets. Public humanities programs can be targeted to strengthen and sharpen the global vision of local leadership, to strengthen the power of local educational institutions and resources to become globally competitive, and to develop greater strategic focus for cultural institutions and programs as an infrastructure for continuous learning opportunities in the local area. By strategically linking and building leadership, educational, and cultural capacity in a locality, the public humanities can contribute directly to the viability of communities and regions in the new global order. **Humanities-rich communities that succeed in linking leadership, education, and cultural assets are more competitive and so offer the prospect of a greater state of well-being for citizens.**

Figure 4 models this need to link assets in leadership, education, and culture. Globally competitive communities create virtuous spirals of growth from the linking of leadership vision with the educational and cultural assets of a region or a community. As a result, human, intellectual, and spiritual capital are strengthened, and this, in turn, fuels economic prosperity and creates the economic resources to feed back into the system. The cycle becomes self-reinforcing and stronger over time in vibrant, sustainable communities.

The model in Figure 4 is read from left to right. Beginning with the region's "story," or self-image, and basic "hardware assets" on the left, the model goes on to illustrate the linkage of leadership, education, and culture and the outcomes for human capital and economic prosperity. The story of a region or a community is a boundary condition on the system. The story of a region may be true or false, may represent an overblown vision of the region's accomplishments, or may represent a deficient self-image and underappreciation of the region's accomplishments. The story may be more mythic or folkloric than scientific, but it still exerts an effect on the region's capacity for direction and positive change. In general, the more vibrant regions tend to have an optimistic story that emphasizes the region's achievements and projects a sense that anything can be accomplished, if attempted seriously. Vibrant regions tend to feel that they compare favorably with other regions and that they are "destinations," not simply transit locations or points to somewhere else.

The "hardware" assets of a region are represented as basic system conditions in this model. Infrastructure for transportation, security, public services, and so forth, constitutes a set of basics that any community or region is simply expected to have. In the past, these constituted some degree of competitive advantage, but no longer. The sources of global competitive advantage, as Porter and others point out, now reside in the community "software," or what we have described as the virtuous spiral dynamics linking leadership, education, and culture. Extending the computer analogy, the patterns, plans, and "codes" that link these assets operate like a software program for the community, using the basic infrastructure and the region's story like hardware. The outputs of this software are human and economic capital growth, as illustrated in Figure 4.

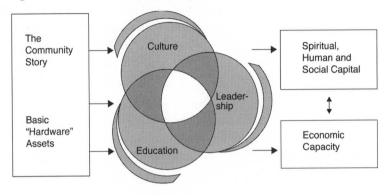

Figure 4. Community Basics and Their Outputs

Ed Morrison of the Indiana Humanities Council has developed the diagram in Figure 5 to illustrate more detail of the social dynamic outlined earlier

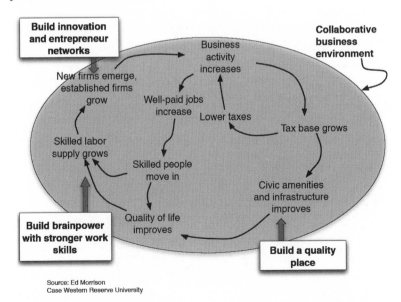

Figure 5. The Prosperous Cycle of Economic Development

Morrison's models identified three key systems that relate to the three in Figure 5. In Morrison's terms, "entrepreneurship and innovation" relates to leadership, "brainpower and skills" relates to education and continuous learning, and "quality place" relates to culture. As these three systems strengthen and interact, a seemingly unrelated set of subcycles emerge and strengthen the larger assets. For example, lower taxes increase business activity, which increases the tax base. This in turn builds more cultural and civic assets, and better-educated, talented people move in, thus improving the quality of products, quality of life, and opportunities for further growth.

By the same token, communities that do not develop the leadership networks, intellectual capital, and cultural capital necessary to add value may find themselves in "death spirals." Death-spiral dynamics are extremely difficult to reverse once a critical point has been reached. The dynamics become self-reinforcing and rapidly deteriorating. In the context of globalization, these death spirals may occur more rapidly than they did in the past, when communities were more insulated from global competition and trends. In the past, communities died over decades or centuries. Today, that time scale is shrinking.

Morrison has developed the model shown in Figure 6 of local death-spiral dynamics.

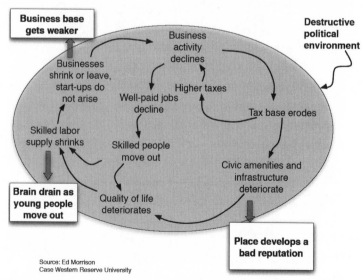

Source: Ed Morrison
Case Western Reserve University

Figure 6. The Downward Cycle of Economic Development

Morrison's field-tuned research argues that creating the right dynamics in a region to support growth must be based on an inclusive civic dialogue and space. In the past, corporate leaders provided primary leadership for economic development, and the private interests of these leaders were usually also part of the equation of growth and plan for the future. Today, global competition makes it necessary to broaden this leadership and broaden the set of resources brought to bear. For example, investment in building a new, innovative company in a region may be lost down the road if the region does not provide competitive educational and cultural resources to retain the talented workers needed by the industry. Such companies may be attracted to more competitive regions, once initial success is achieved. To avoid such long-term depletion of investment and talent, regions must build inclusive civic leadership and dialogue to enable the investments of business, government, and the nonprofit sectors to become aligned and strategic across sectors. This, in turn, requires communities and leaders to invent a "new form of civic discourse" and to "reinvent the civic space."

The humanities could and should play a creative role in convening cross-sector leaders and helping to build the inclusive civic dialogue that makes such alignment possible. In general, this need points further to a potential expanding leadership role for the entire nonprofit sector. Unlike corporations, which can relocate, nonprofits are indigenous. Unlike government, which carries the benefit and cost of legislative and coercive power, the nonprofit sector is not mandated to lead. However, given the need for leadership that can be trusted to convene across sectors and to help lead without its own agenda, the nonprofit sector is especially structured to provide such nonpartisan inclusive leadership. A tremendous opportunity exists for the humanities to play a vital, new role as a thought leader in creating a new civility for regions and communities.

A new type of leadership is needed to make local regions globally competitive. At the level of globalization, a new cosmopolitan leadership is also needed for business, government, and nonprofit enterprises. An informed understanding and empathy for other cultures and an understanding of history, languages, religious institutions, and ideas are important for today's leaders, as well as technical expertise in various fields.

A primary question of empowerment in our times will concern the interaction of the modern state and corporation in relation to other social institutions, such as families, schools, churches and other religious organizations, the arts, and voluntary organizations. What will the public humanities have to say about the structure of social life and the role of leaders in the coming decades? Further, globalization and technology empower individuals more than in the past and hence raise the consequences of personal character and the choices individuals make in "leading" their lives. Differentiated societies are producing a new philosophy embracing a more pluralistic, secularized world and an integrated global economy. Businesses are partnering with nonprofit organizations and with those who can help to create new markets as fully responsible societal leaders. Now a reality are the rise of corporate statesmanship and, in certain polities, the emergence of business-based political entities or advocacy, including political candidates with business but no prior political experience. Who will our new leaders be? How will they be educated? What appreciation will they have for the humanities, and how grounded will they be in the liberal arts? Will the rise of science and technology as new literacies force out the old paradigms? The question of values-based leadership is as critical today as at any time in the past. Which values and norms will prevail? Who decides? And ultimately, Who rules?

The integrated global economy depends upon a climate of predictability, trust, partnership, and shared values. There is always a balance to be struck between change and continuity. The greatest part of wisdom is keeping the most valuable elements of the past. Leadership is the key to the mastery of change. And organizational leadership implies not only continuity with the highest standard of ethical norms and professional skill but also spiritual capital. *Ethics* is therefore taking on an even greater role in a world of intricate and cross-cultural relationships. The future is seen as the responsibility of organizations we inhabit and their leaders, whom we choose. They have the power to analyze the facts and to establish the practical implications of ideals. They have the freedom to quickly adjust policies, to mobilize resources, and, most important, to create wealth. The unfinished agenda of the past century beckons the international leaders of tomorrow. New definitions and horizons of leadership will arise in every kind of organization to meet these new challenges. This new leadership is likely to be more global, more diverse, less gender dominant, and educationally and linguistically both extremely literate and numerate. Will they be educated in or disposed toward the humanities? With the growing interconnectedness of cultures, what other framework is more relevant?

We have seen earlier that the humanities were created as a program to prepare leaders for democratic communities in ancient Greece. The issue remains the same, but the scale is vastly greater today. Democratic leadership and self-governance (liberty) in a small, self-contained *polis* and democratic leadership and liberty in "global-local communities" are alike in purpose but different in the scale of responsibilities and impact. **The urgency is the same: to cultivate the potential for enlightened and responsible leadership appropriate to the given context of action. Envisioning and designing the curriculum for global leadership is at the top of the agenda for humanities organizations today.**

The academic community addresses this issue in the context of formal education, as recently outlined by Sheldon Rothblatt in the *Living Arts*, a study conducted on the future of the liberal arts for the Association of American Colleges and Universities.[2] The field of the public humanities, on the other hand, is responsible for designing and supporting programming beyond the academy to enlighten and support leadership. Although many promising steps are being taken to reconnect the liberal arts and humanities with formal education for tomorrow's leadership and with existing leaders, this remains an area in need of far more creative work and invention. Today, more than ever, leadership is confronted by change across cultures and fields. How are leaders to be prepared to lead and manage this rate of change?

"Leaders always have to balance the demand for continuity against the demand for change," according to Jerry Mechling of the Kennedy School of Government at Harvard University.[3] But today, he notes, "the change agenda is where leadership must focus." A "culture of change" is deep, he further argues, because "culture is deep. Culture is how we know things work without being told; it is our norms, our values, our instinctive procedures. Culture does not change quickly." Hence, today, leadership is key to a culture of change. Developing learning organizations that can adapt to change is the central issue. To help leaders with this role, Mechling has recommended eight strategies to develop a culture of change under two broad priorities.

1. Plan innovation, implement, and measure results.

Develop an innovations-oriented investment portfolio. Make the idea of change a priority—and fund it. As business, government, and nonprofits budget resources, part of the portfolio has to be the change agenda, investment for the future. The higher risk, higher return elements will be the most critical things to do. Budget for innovation and risk.

Focus the portfolio on global knowledge work. The driver of economic growth is knowledge work; this is global. The change is not limited to production. Even office work has become global.

Take advantage of the information highway. Virtual integration and access offering are the way work will be done soon. Use the Internet and new communications capabilities to reform the public, private, and non-profit institutions and their business relationships with others.

Measure what you do. Priorities and plans are not taken seriously until they are measured. Innovation and dynamic change need to be measured. At the same time, innovation does not occur without lots of mistakes. Clear measurement of progress along with a tolerance for mistakes are both necessary in a context of change and innovation.

2. Build innovative infrastructure.

Act regionally and across sectors. Regions are the new operating system for progress because the resources needed to compete are spread across sectors and geography. To act regionally requires consolidation of local governments and new venues for bringing the public, private and non-profit sectors together to plan and act.

Extend business-relevant education throughout life. Create the educational programs and structures to provide business-relevant learning throughout a lifetime and your workforce will innovate and create wealth.

Reform government budgeting to enable innovation. Government budgets miss the high-value investments - particularly innovative technology-related investments -- because they tend to be short-term and constructed program by program. Without reform in the budgeting process in the public sector, government will consistently miss the high-value opportunities.

Provide safety nets to buffer the turbulence that accompanies change. We have done a reasonable job in the 20th century of balancing the continued pressures of getting rid of unneeded jobs and being humane about providing safety nets to dislocated workers. Without a sense of community responsibility, we will not do well.[4]

In the previous chapter, we examined ways in which leadership is like a work of art in that it demands that leaders develop an "artist's eye" for identifying high-value concepts and trends from a vast amount of information. In other words, a key leadership skill for the future is an ability to pick out meaningful and valuable ideas from data and to create something new that other people want. Leadership today is focused on the change agenda, which requires leaders who are highly self-defined and comfortable in contexts of ambiguity, even anxiety. Friedman's criteria for nonanxious leaders, cited in the previous chapter, is a good thumbnail of this leadership profile.

In this chapter, we have looked at the context in which leadership operates today, noting that corporate, government, and nonprofit leaders operate in both global and local contexts. This also demands a new set of skills for leaders: a keen appreciation for local qualities and assets, together with an ability to project them onto the global stage. Because major forces today are driven at the global level, not the national level, local communities and regions may become trapped relatively quickly in downward spirals and decay. To prevent this, leaders will be called upon to create a new "civic space" in which other leaders from all sectors can be mobilized quickly to connect and strengthen local assets into open networks of innovation that have global value and competitiveness. This new civic leadership is critical to the future viability of communities and regions. Since the humanities were created to define and transmit leadership in democratic communities, the humanities have a large new role to play in the development of these new leadership virtues.

Notes

1. Michael Porter, *The Competitive Advantage of Nations* (New York: Free Press, 1998).
2. Sheldon Rothblatt, Living Arts: *Comparative and Historical Reflections on Liberal Education* (Washington, DC: Association of American Colleges and Universities, 2003).
3. Jerry Mechling, "A Framework for Dynamic Change," 2004 *Leadership Summit Report: A Call to Action* (Indianapolis: Indiana Humanities Council, 2004), p. 8.
4. Ibid., pp. 6–7.

8

Finance and New Roles for Civil Society

I T IS A TRUISM these days that money makes the world go
around. For centuries, however, money was viewed with con-
tempt or disdain: something to be left to the usurers, to char-
latans changing money in the Temple, or to the lower classes
involved in commercial affairs or trading in the Agora. The early
philosophers often looked down at those involved in business.
Even the early Church fathers, no doubt influenced by injunc-
tions against usury in the Torah and by Hellenistic philosophy,
saw money, or at least the love of money, as evil—something to
be rendered unto Caesar. Christ said in parables that it was hard-
er for a rich man to enter heaven than for a camel to go through
the eye of a needle. St. Francis of Assisi, as did many in the
monastic tradition, renounced wealth altogether. The papal
authorities banned all sorts of commercial activity, tried to determine just prices, and had no place for interest taking. It was not
until St. Thomas and the Schoolmen that, in a more enterprising
time and with a feudal society needing more resources, the
Church and medieval society began to make peace with com-

merce. Did they realize that commerce and community and communion all had the same Latin root?

Flash ahead into the present, and we witness a radically different world and economic situation. Material prosperity is spreading rapidly, and commercial activity has vaulted to the top of the pecking order. Everyone, it seems, wants to be rich or famously rich. Rock stars, athletes, CEOs, and moguls of every stripe are paid extravagantly. Countries measure their status by every kind of statistic but none more demonstrably than on the altar of gross domestic product. The financial competitiveness of nations is a game with real consequences for entire populations. Is there a country or a region that is not seeking foreign direct investment? Is there a standard higher than ROI? As the London department store Harrods says, almost everything is for sale, and we will find it for you. More time and effort are expended on financial advice, career planning, and credit these days than on any other facet of our existence. Finances have become the number-one cause for marital discord and divorce.

Much has been made of low savings rates and of pension and retirement plans going bust. Wall Street waits on every word that comes out of the Federal Reserve chairman's breath. Whisper numbers circulate on Wall Street about company financials on a quarterly basis. Even universities and foundations are dependent on the market performance for their growing endowments. It would be foolish to leave finances to the financers. Too much depends on budgets, expenditures, and lifestyles to put off financing the future. Companies cannot grow without access to capital markets. Government programs are dependent on internal revenue collections. And the social sector is almost entirely a captive to the growth of wealth that yields charity.

Most nonprofit organizations have come to money matters lately and with some hesitancy. They do not generally have professional money people and often focus more on their missions and doing service than on measures of productivity. The stereotypes of big business or the rich and the social sector—one with the hand outstretched; the other, with the hand on the wallet—

rings too true. This phobia about finance should be overcome with sound judgment and a realization that in a prosperous economy, particularly in a global setting, we all have to take finances seriously. It is no longer simply an accountant's job or the job of businesspeople. Even in the nonprofit organization today, there are stricter rules on reporting and governance and for transactions. Every organization must know and live by these new rules and even exceed the minimum responses in order to earn a Good Housekeeping seal of approval.

In this chapter, we examine new ways to finance the humanities; the changing roles of government, business, and the nonprofit sectors; and ideas to create a positive new definition of the "nonprofit" sector. Finally, evoking earlier discussions of the "spiritual" basis of capital, we offer a brief view of economics as an important and undervalued form of humanism.

Financing the Humanities

How will the humanities finance themselves in this new world? In the past, state entitlements and government funds provided a foundation of support. Budgets grew, and organizations had slightly more money to spend every year. There was little need for imagination or creative budgeting or for additional financing from other sources. How quickly things have changed.

The state alone in most cases is no longer able or willing to keep pace with new demands and has in many places and instances cut budgets, especially for the arts and humanities. More and more institutions are calling on their publics—or, to use a previously forbidden word, customers—to pay for services and goods either on a contributory scheme or in a very real market, competing with real for-profit companies. PBS faces the History Channel and Discovery, *National Geographic* has imitators, private museums have opened, Disney has history-based theme parks, and the list goes on. How can poorly funded, often small, understaffed public humanities groups and agencies compete or thrive in such a world? Will they be able to meet the challenge?

The answer, in a nutshell, is no, unless they change. That is, there is likely to be a shrinking humanities sector in the future. This is in fact already the situation. Increases in federal and state funding for the humanities have not kept pace with inflation, and so the field is already in a shrinking economic sphere. What can be done to turn the situation around?

The humanities are in need of a creative renewal grounded in the pursuit of happiness. That is, as has been argued throughout this book, **the humanities need to be reengaged with intellectual renewal and with science, the arts, and religion in a constructive effort to envision and articulate for the broad public a positive vision of a future of human flourishing.** A mission based almost entirely in contrarian and marginal viewpoints will not engage the public sufficiently to engender growing economic investment. Competition for investments is increasing. Hence, the criteria for investing resources are becoming more rigorous and targeted. As societies look more and more for solutions-oriented opportunities in which to invest funds, the humanities must find a genuine area of need in which to contribute. As we have seen, there are many such needs, and, as the popularity of humanities enterprises, such as the History Channel, and the amazing attraction of a wide array of self-help and spiritual advisors and speakers show, there is an enormous appetite for humanities content—as long as the content does not deny the value of everything constituting human life. So, step one is to articulate a positive, creative vision and mission.

In fact, there is a critical need for insight from the humanities in developing a clearer and more coherent understanding of the entire nonprofit sector. The nonprofit sector is recognized as the third sector of the economy, alongside the private business sector and the public governmental sector. Unlike these two sectors, however, the nonprofit sector has no core definitive role, as the name itself reveals. This third sector of the economy is not organized around profit, as is the private sector, and is not a part of government and so is called either nonprofit or nongovernmental. These titles say what the sector is not, but what is it? What kind of activity requires the specific organizational structure of the third sector, and what kinds of resources should be invested and how? We return to this topic later in this chapter with a look at how civil society should be organized in the context of globalization.

For now, the best evidential advice may be illustrative. Here are five ways some public humanities groups have been reinventing their financial prospects. They suggest ways that the humanities need to find new financial mechanisms that connect to commerce and public support, as well as charitable contributions.

1. *Diversified fund raising.* A public media outlet decided to take in more than half of its revenues from the public and strategized to offer a program benefit to individuals who pledged larger gifts on a recurring basis.

2. *Sponsored underwriting.* A state council commenced a Leadership Council and Leadership Summit annual event that was financed by twin revenue streams from paying attendees and major underwriting from sponsoring companies.

3. *Partnering with corporations.* A music center started a royalty-paying arrangement with a major corporation for intellectual property it owned and for which there existed a sizeable market.

4. *Pursuing earned revenues by selling more goods and services.* A consortium of museums banded together to sell their individual products and wares through a national department/specialty retail store and online.

5. *Implementing effective investment strategies.* A university employed state-of-the-art diversified financial investment schemes, including hedge funds, alternative investments, and venture capital, to grow its endowment by record amounts over a five-year period.

There are, it is said, only a few things you can't live with or live without. Finances are certainly one of them. The public humanities as a project will succeed or fail on the basis of its content first and foremost, but it will have greater effect and extended reach if it is more inventive and entrepreneurial in its approaches to financing its considerable store of treasures.

Finance and Civil Society

The dynamics and structures of finance bring to light important structural and operational features of society. Three broad social sectors related to revenue sources and fiscal structure can be discerned.

The first, foundational sector is the *private sector*. In a free society, it is appropriate that the largest single sector should be allocated to private affairs, contracts, pledges, and activities. The private corporate sector, with its business, finance, legal, and market functions, is designed to be optimally efficient and effective in satisfying human desires. We use the term *desire* rather than *needs* intentionally. No adequate definition of needs is possible, because, like atoms, there turns out to be no such thing as an absolutely ultimate, indivisible need. All needs are flexible and open to further reduction and shaping. Needs are defined within some context of available resources and admit of continuous fine-tuning. Is a measured quantity of rice or beans right to meet a need? How are they prepared? Desires, on the other hand, are definable, measurable, and by nature infinitely malleable. Commerce aims at satisfying desires and seldom bothers itself with the effort to define needs.

Human desires are endless and admit of continuous alteration. In the context of free markets, business aims at satisfying as many diverse and changing desires as possible. The endless productivity of markets, thus, is a kind of map, or projection, of the endless drama of desire. A free market produces an incredible variety of goods and services, from the sublime to the ridiculous, because the sector is designed to measure and respond to desire. The exchange of goods and services that arises as a result of the free enterprise to satisfy desires creates economic value. Value arises from the quantity and quality of exchange. Commerce, hence, is the source of wealth and prosperity in society.

The private sector is now the ultimate source of economic value and resources among the three sectors. In past times, the public sector was the primary generator of the wealth of nations. Through war and imperial expansion, nations increased their wealth by acquiring additional land and natural resources. Today, in contrast, economic growth is based on the value generated through innovation and the exchange of goods and services in free markets regulated by the rule of law. Thus, the sector of private commerce and finance has become the engine of economic growth. This is taken to an even higher level with the advent and growth of globalization.

The public sector is dependent on the private sector for resources. The resources of government are generated through taxation, not through the creation of new wealth or economic value.

Although the private sector and the public sector have reliable mechanisms for producing revenues to finance activities of their sectors, the third sector does not. The third sector is dependent on both the private and public sectors. Further, although there is growing expertise and technical knowledge to guide investment in business and in government spending for infrastructure and security, there is no comparable expertise and theory to guide investment in the nonprofit sector. Instead, this sector appeals to charitable and philanthropic impulses, which are largely unregulated by any overarching concept of the role of the third sector. Of course, there are development consultants and accepted strategies and practices for capital campaigns and for soliciting funds, and many foundations and corporations have developed formal procedures and criteria for their philanthropic activity. But these are piecemeal solutions, and on the whole, the sector remains in a relatively primitive, unscientific stage of investment theory. It is not terribly innovative or venture oriented.

A full human life and human society achieves more than the exchange of goods and services and the satisfaction of desires. In addition to exchange, social functions are needed to ensure the rule of law and to harness human energies to serve in the public interest. The public, governmental sector exists to ensure security, order, and public goods and services. The funding mechanism for the private sector is commercial exchange; the funding mechanism for the public sector depends on the commercial sector and takes the form of consensual taxation and levies, as noted.

The nonprofit, or nongovernmental, sector is currently problematic. At present, the third sector has no clearly defined positive function; hence, its title states what it is *not*—not commercial, not government. This negative definition suggests that the third sector is a sort of stopgap, which historically has often been the case. The ad hoc nature of the sector is also apparent in the fact that no reliable mechanism for revenue generation is tied to the sector. Commerce and government have clear mechanisms for generating the revenues that support their activities and permit them to achieve scale. The nonprofit sector, however, has several partial revenue sources, none of which are designed to bring nonprofit service, as a social good, to scale or with regularity.

Nonprofit organizations may generate revenues from commerce by creating a for-profit subsidiary or entering into joint ventures with corporations. Nonprofits may also receive public funding. Third, nonprofits may generate revenues from individual charitable donations, foundations, or corporate grants or sponsorships.

Perhaps foundations are the most likely area for a rational funding pattern for nonprofits. Foundations are themselves nonprofits and are established to support the work carried out by nonprofits. Foundations serve as a revenue source within the third sector, and nonprofits serve as the operations and service provider of the third sector; foundations and nonprofits are two sides of the same coin. However, foundations and nonprofits do not typically work together in a strategic, transparent manner. Foundations create their own strategic focus and framing of social needs internally, without input from nonprofit service providers. Although foundations and nonprofits need each other to function, they do not collaborate formally to define the strategic direction both will pursue. The divide between foundations and nonprofits creates complexity and inefficiencies. The operational activity of the nonprofit sector is essentially separated from the revenue sources of the sector. Hence, unlike in the private sector, revenues and operations are disconnected.

Recent well-publicized research forecasts an enormous growth in revenues for the nonprofit sector over the next decades, something over $40 trillion, as vast wealth is passed from one generation to the next. The prospect of this infusion of resources is a further good reason to rethink the relation between foundations and nonprofits and ways to improve effectiveness, reduce duplications of effort, and invest rationally in scalable efforts with valuable and measured outcomes. Research further shows that individuals are by far the largest source of contributed resources to nonprofits, primarily religious institutions or institutions from which they receive direct benefits (e.g., schools, hospitals, and service organizations that they use). Foundations are second, and corporations are last, after legacy gifts from personal estates. Although corporations control the vast amount of private wealth in the economy, they are the smallest investors in the third sector. This fact represents an opportunity. Strategic thinking in the nonprofit sector over joint-venture opportunities with the corporate sector has the potential to open the door to greatly expanded resources for the sector. But the joint investment would have to have benefits for both sides.

Reenvisioning the Nonprofit Sector

Within civil society, the third sector needs to be reenvisioned to have its own distinct, positive function to fulfill. The third sector needs to move beyond being "nonprofit" or "nongovernmental" to become a positively understood sector with its own clear function and mechanism for revenues. **In a global knowledge-based economy driven by innovation, the nonprofit sector needs to be rethought, and the humanities should play a critical role in helping to define both purpose and strategies.**

Lester Salamon, Director of the Center for Civil Society Studies at Johns Hopkins University Institute for Policy Studies, recently noted ten myths that are relevant to a rethinking about the nonprofit sector. Dr. Salamon's comments centered on research conducted in thirty-seven countries worldwide and challenged a number of the myths that plague the third sector. His comments were originally presented at the Imagine Canada Symposium "Learning from the World: Canada's Charitable and Nonprofit Sector through a Global Lens" and are summarized here.[1] They are most illuminating.

Myth 1: Civil society is made up only of NGOs. The third sector tends to focus on what is different instead of on commonalities and tends to use words that obscure functional activity. The use of the term *NGO* is an example.

Myth 2: The civil society sector is a marginal economic actor. In the thirty-seven countries measured by the Hopkins Institute, the civil society sector employs 4.5% of total employees in the workforce and spends $1.33 trillion. Measured by gross domestic product, the third sector is the fifth-largest industry in the world and employs eight times the number of employees as the utilities sector.

Myths 3 and 4: Civil society organizations are chiefly an American phenomenon and are not present in Europe, where reliance on government is greater. The truth is that civil society is a global phenomenon.

Myths 5 and 6: Volunteers play a more important role in the civil society workforce in developing than in developed countries; paid staff drives out reliance on volunteers. The worldwide average shows nearly half, or 44%, of the workforce in civil society organizations are volunteers; this statistic does not vary widely with wealthier versus less-wealthy countries. Volunteering is a social act that needs to be mobilized, and research proves that an effective volunteer effort significantly benefits from the presence of paid staff to provide structure.

Myth 7: The civil society sector is engaged mostly in the provision of services. Civil society sector organizations act a vehicle for the expression of a variety of human values, including cultural and religious values, and serve to establish trust, bonds of reciprocity, and the social capital essential to a healthy society.

Myths 8 and 9: Philanthropy is the chief source of civil society revenue. The global average of civil society sector revenue breaks down as follows: government contributions, 35% of revenue; fees and charges, 53% of revenue; and philanthropy, only 12% of revenue.

Myth 10: The civil society sector is growing at a slower rate than the private business sector. Employment statistics measured in eight countries between 1990 and 1995 demonstrate that the sector experienced 24% growth compared to an average overall employment growth of 8%.

According to this report, the world is "experiencing a global associational revolution and there is a worldwide search on for new models to effectively manage civil societies." Salamon also noted the important rise in social entrepreneurs (wealthy individuals, lawyers, artists, engineers, physicists) who consciously turn to civil society organizations to give meaning to their lives. These new developments, together with the common myths and misperceptions, underscore the need to rethink the sector extensively. In particular, Salamon observed the need for new interoperability among sectors, stressing that "we simply cannot go it alone, we have prided ourselves on our independence for too long. The key to the future is cross-sectored initiatives." To create this type of large-scale, cross-sector work requires an overall theory in which to embed the role of the sectors in society.

Plato's *Republic* is suggestive of a way this might be accomplished. Plato and Aristotle both understood human beings to be complex, dynamic agents whose creative energies fall into three broad categories of drive. The first and largest set of drives is directed toward the appetites, the desires satisfied through consumption and possession. The second center of energy Plato called "noble passion," or the desire to protect and serve the community. The third center of energy for both Plato and Aristotle is intellectual and spiritual. The goal of this energetic drive is wisdom, a creative intellectual aesthetic that enables the recognition of good form and good order in things and people. As noted earlier, this activity is also an expression of the pursuit of happiness, or a well-ordered personal life.

Using this as a guide, the three sectors of civil society could be mapped along similar lines. The private sector is designed to provide the social structures to satisfy appetites for possessions and consumption. The public sector provides a range of action for the "noble passions" of protection and service to the community through government service, legislation, military service, and other services designed to protect and serve. Finally, the third sector could be understood as the social structure designed to support the flowering of intellectual and spiritual energies that sustain the pursuit of happiness. The present nonprofit sector already has some of these features; religious institutions, universities and schools, and art and cultural organizations are all organized as nonprofits. What has been missing is a general understanding that the sector functions primarily to express intellectual and spiritual values and to provide a source of wisdom that explicitly feeds back into the community in a "virtuous spiral" of learning, growth, and innovation.

In order to be scalable and to justify sufficient investment, the nonprofit sector needs to be rationalized in some way so that investment can be clearly tied to desired outcomes that can be measured. The origins of the nonprofit sector go back to agrarian and tribal economies. In these contexts, resources were clearly directed toward acts of charity, usually tied to religious communities and practices. Over time, early charitable institutions were formed around these practices: temple, church, hospitals, and various charities for the poor and hungry. Education was the next major early nonprofit institution. The ancient schools of Plato, Aristotle, the Stoics, Epicureans, and others received gifts of land

and money from wealthy patrons, and this practice continued and expanded as support for universities and schools from medieval to contemporary times. In these economic settings, the third sector was closely linked to religious and educational activities, and these continue to be the primary institutions to benefit from charitable donations.

Intermediate institutions and voluntary associations in particular have played and continue to play a significant role in American culture. Tocqueville recognized that voluntary associations were part of the genius of American culture.[2] Nonprofits are a perfect example of voluntary associations. The great threat to the existence of and the functioning of voluntary associations has been the growth of the state. As the state has been expected to take on more and more functions previously handled by voluntary associations, those associations and their wellsprings have begun to dry up. Ironically, universities in general and the humanities in particular, given their general ignorance and disdain for economics, have endorsed public policies that promote the growth of the state and the decline of voluntary associations. They have been engaged, in short, in a slow form of institutional suicide.

Economics as Humanism: Beyond Winners and Losers

For most of history, economics has been seen as a field of ultimate winners and losers. The economic pie has been understood as limited by its very nature; hence, in this view, when someone gets more and more of the economic pie, the result is less for everyone else. Thus, wars and pillage have been primary engines of economic growth for societies of the past, as the great museums of Europe attest. Efforts to ameliorate the winner/loser structure of economics has led to the ideas and policies of distributive justice, an effort on the part of the public sector to prevent the private sector from allocating almost all the economic pie to the winners.

Robert Heilbroner's 1965 book *The Limits of American Capitalism* drew further implications from this model of economics and argued that, with limited natural resources available in the world for making goods, economic growth could not continue. This conclusion seemed to underscore the coming urgency of redistribution of wealth as the expansion of the American economic pie gradually began to shrink, like a dying big bang, and so to make the limits of the overall pie even more starkly evident. The closing chapter of Heilbroner's book raised one intriguing alternative—the infinite boundaries of the mind and imagination might provide an alternative arena for the American impulse to expand and seek more. The mind and culture, Heilbroner argued, unlike natural materials, such as iron, coal, and oil, are infinitely expansive; this domain, he noted, admits of unending expansion. As he wrote:

> could there be an equivalent of that powerfully disintegrative and yet constitutive force in our day—a force sufficiently overwhelming to render impotent the citadel of capitalism and yet as irresistibly attractive to its masters as the earlier current of change was to feudalism? There is such a force, and it already bulks very large within our world, where it is cumulatively and irreversibly altering the social system even more rapidly than did the process of monetization during the medieval era. This revolutionary power is the veritable explosion of organized knowledge and its applied counterpart, scientific technology, in modern times.[3]

Heilbroner did not realize that he had in fact anticipated the new frontier of economic activity rather than its final terminus. The knowledge economy does move beyond the limits of the old industrial economy by harnessing the innovative powers of the mind and culture as economic drivers.

This new economy permits us to foresee a future in which potentially every human being can contribute and participate in an ever-expanding economic pie. We are now just beginning to grasp the concept of economics as a win-win game rather than as a win-lose game. From such a point of view, humanistic values that respect and defend the dignity and rights of each person to economic well-being and the goals of commercial success in the knowledge economy converge. In this context, the universal spread of free markets, the rule of law, and private commerce are practical methods for accomplishing some of the goals of classical humanistic vision. **It is increasingly critical, therefore, that leaders in the private sector understand and articulate the larger humanistic goals of commerce and that leaders in the humanities and nonprofit sector come to understand the practical methods and rationales of knowledge-based economics.** The old rift between wealth and wisdom is closing.

The relation of money to wisdom and the spiritual dimensions of life have been unclear and problematic in the past, as noted earlier in this chapter. New studies of capital, from the standpoint of spiritual issues, however, are becoming an important new area of study. Clearly, money is more than a valuable commodity, or a thing to hoard under the mattress. Money is fluid and dynamic; it fuels activities across the whole spectrum of human society and life. From one point of view, money is a metric that serves to manage and govern flows of energy and activity in society. Money exercises a type of governance and homeostatic control over activities and creates hierarchies of differentiated skills, relations, and work in order to leverage these skill sets and relations for greater results. **If personal happiness consists of the well-fitted energies of individual character, perhaps it is not too much to think that social happiness might consist of the well-fitted arrangement of differentiated skills and actions made possible through the mechanisms of humanistic finance and money.**

Robert Wright of Princeton University and author of *Nonzero: The Logic of Human Destiny*, wrote recently that:

> Capitalism's pre-eminence as a wealth generator means that every tyrant has to either embrace free markets or fall slowly into economic oblivion; but for markets to work, citizens need access to information technology and the freedom to use it— and that means having political power.

> This link between economic and political liberty has been extolled...for centuries, but the microelectronic age has strengthened it. Even China's deftly capitalist-yet-authoritarian

government—which embraces technology while blocking Web sites…is doomed to fail in the long run.[4]

Wright's point clarifies a further dimension of the humanism of economic growth. The expansion of commerce through capital markets is a carrier of the rule of law, as we have seen, and even more important, a carrier of civil society and democracy. The moral justification and ground for capitalism is inscribed in this historical narrative of expanding civil and political health and liberty. This perspective must today become integral to all understandings of commerce and enterprise, both to give it moral weight and a moral compass and to meet objections of those who perceive capitalist economics simply in terms of materialism and wealth.

Notes

1. Lester Salamon, "Ten Myths of Global Civil Society," *The Contributor* (Toronto: AFP Greater Toronto monthly newsletter, April 2005).
2. Alexis de Tocqueville, *Democracy in America*, rev. ed. (New York: Signet Books, 2001).
3. Robert Heilbroner, *The Limits of American Capitalism* (New York: Torchbooks, 1965), pp. 113–114.
4. Robert Wright, "The Market Shall Set You Free," *New York Times*, January 25, 2005.

9

Governance, Transparency, Civil Society, and Justice

I N THE PAST DECADE, a plethora of new laws, rules, and
cases have made companies, cultural organizations and
other nonprofits, governmental and international agencies,
and their executives increasingly accountable for the manner in
which they manage their organizations. The spread of higher
standards for corporate governance can be seen from the passage
of new securities laws in the United States to promulgation of the
Cadbury Report in the United Kingdom. In the nonprofit and
governmental sectors, concerns about the Red Cross's handling
of the 9/11 funds, the government's handling of the relief efforts
after hurricanes Katrina and Rita, and the United Nation's handling of the Oil for Food program in Iraq highlight the ubiquity
of concerns regarding governance and transparency and their
impact on all sectors.

Although the leading-edge developments in governance and
transparency are taking place primarily in the corporate sector,
the issues are equally important for government and for nonprof-

its. Global competition for investment funds means that every enterprise will be under increased scrutiny for performance at all levels, from governance to service.

Hence, it is important to place the issues of governance and transparency for nonprofits and the humanities into the broader, global corporate context and the global competition for funds. In the future, the governance and function of nonprofits will be shaped increasingly by pressures and developments from around the world. Like their for-profit counterparts, nonprofits will be impacted by global dynamics that affect governance, social responsibilities, and ground rules for global investment and accountability, whether for profit or for human development. This will help to explain the underlying reasons for rethinking governance for the nonprofit in general and the humanities in particular, perhaps suggesting some analogies and lessons from the corporate experience that may be highly relevant.

Higher standards for governance and additional rules bring increasing responsibility and liability. In the United States, approximately half of all suits against corporate boards are filed by shareholders, and shareholders' claims cost many millions in settlement or judgment. Numerous cases have been filed overseas as well. The U.S.-based scandals of Enron, Adelphia, and WorldCom, among others, have brought governance and transparency to the forefront of public awareness. Although nonprofits are not sued by disgruntled board members or the public, governance problems and a lack of transparency can result in lost contributions or the demise of the organization. United Way of America, for example, is still working to overcome governance and transparency problems from more than a decade ago. For the humanities, the challenge by the 92nd Congress to the charter and funding for the National Endowment for the Humanities and for the fifty-six state and territorial councils was in part a challenge over the governance and transparency of the organizations in terms of the nonpartisan nature of their programs and missions. Neither the NEH nor the councils have regained funding levels lost from the challenge, much less kept pace with inflation or increased public support.

Over the past few years, a disturbing number of nonprofits have been the subject of embarrassing and problematic failures: inquiries into investment irregularities, ethical lapses, and outright scandals. Everything from financial irregularities to burnouts by chief executive officers, self-enrichment by trustees to misallocation of donated funds, and excessive compensation arrangements to fraud have been the ruin of many organizations. So many nonprofits have lost their way, beset by loss of membership or audience, budget deficits, or irrelevancy of mission, that it is impossible to even keep track. But scores of other nonprofits have thrived, have never been in better shape, and are ever stronger. Why do some nonprofits have success and others such difficulty? Although leadership is crucial, the key reason boils down to good governance.

To quote a recent report on the subject:

> Nonprofits with superior governing boards tend, on balance, to be far more effective, focused and financially sound than those with weak, confused or inappropriate ones. They are far less likely to run into major disputes with their chief executive officers, have conflicts of interest or self-enrichment problems or experience significant, continuing budgetary woes. . . . Superbly governed nonprofits continuously take the long view: they are clear about, and believe wholeheartedly in, their missions; they think and act strategically, focusing on the future rather than the past or present; and they look regularly for independent external validation of the relevance, quality and effectiveness of programs and initiatives and promptly make appropriate changes and improvements as needed.[1]

The essentials of good nonprofit governance are many but center mostly on the board and a healthy relationship with executive management.

Recent trends have spread around the world as a result of the process of globalization: an increased emphasis on shareholder value (which has a parallel in the nonprofit sector as the value delivered to constituencies as judged by funders and donors), a growing perception of the need for independent directors and committees, and the need for better disclosure of relevant financial information. Some recent developments have added impetus to the corporate governance movement: globalization itself, as action at a distance requires a high level of reliability and transparency; increasing competition for investment funding for all sectors, which increases requirements for performance and assessment; and improved standards of productivity and service in lead organizations, which significantly raises the bar of expectation for all nonprofits, government services, and business. For the private business sector, other contributing factors are a significant increase in mergers, acquisitions, and takeovers around the world; increased aggressiveness by institutional shareholders; the spread of American-style stock options; a reduction in cross-shareholdings and the influence of banks; the growth of venture capital markets; and the issuance by the Organization for Economic Co-operation and Development (OECD) of its "Principles of Corporate Governance." The enactment of the Financial Accounting Standards Board Interpretation rules for nonprofits and the Sarbanes-Oxley Act defining corporate record keeping in the United States and its ramifications on nonprofit and company practice in a host of governance and transparency areas are changing core practices of capitalism and nonprofit finance in the United States and around the world, given the integration of capital markets. Increasingly, boards and CEOs are adapting to the new cry for corporate social responsibility. Those who take a lead in setting high standards for themselves will gain respect and value for their enterprises and organizations.

Where are the public humanities in all this? Did the lack of business ethics emanate in a wider cultural crisis about right and wrong? What sets the framework for the rule and character of organizations and those employed, directing, or leading them? Have the humanities done their part in educating both the public and the leaders of all organizations—corporate, social, and private—about the context, responsibility, and nature of governance? Needless to say, nonprofit organizations have themselves not been immune to the failures of governance or the need for greater transparency. The United Way of America scandal in the

1990s predated the recent wave of complaint about company behavior. Nepotism, cronyism, and conflict of interest are hardly foreigners in the social sector.

One central governance challenge for humanities councils, of which there are fifty-six—one in each state, U.S. territory, and the District of Columbia—concerns academic representation on the boards of councils. Councils were created to form a national network of independent nonprofits anchored in every state and federal jurisdiction to support and stimulate a vibrant civic society and culture. In many states, humanities scholars and administrators make up a significant portion of the board, sometimes up to half; indeed, many councils mandate that a percentage of the board be scholars. A review of grant allocations from councils also shows a large portion of grants awarded to the colleges and universities whose faculty and administration make up a large portion of the board. In many cases, colleges and universities make up the largest sector receiving council grant funding. This creates at least a perceived conflict of interest, since the largest beneficiary of humanities grants is the largest single constituency represented in governance positions on the boards. In the light of increasing emphasis on transparency and governing independence, ad hoc safeguards, such as conflict-of-interest declarations and member abstinence from voting on grants to their own institutions, are unlikely to be viewed as best-of-class standards, since they do not address the structural governance problem. We return to the issue of board governance and the expertise needed by councils and other nonprofits later in the chapter.

The recent governmental focus has been on the audit committee, CEO attestation to financials, and the need for audit committees, in particular, to be both more active and independent. Typical corporate problems have included premature recognition of earnings and the improper use of reserves to manipulate earnings. Such practices conceal what is really happening in any organization. In nonprofits, and for some councils, lack of an independent audit committee has led to opportunities for the staff to disguise the financial condition of the organization from the board. Only when the executive leaves does the real state of affairs come to light. The Blue Ribbon Committee on Improving the Effectiveness of Corporate Audit Committees recommended reinforcing the independence of audit committees and improving their effectiveness. The committee recommended a more stringent definition of "independence." Some observers have asked whether implementation of certain of its recommendations, particularly those that appear to require that audit committee members have detailed technical knowledge of accounting principles, could lead to more litigation against directors. The key to avoiding liability is to have audit committee members who are both independent and active. Conflict of interest is another concern; it has polluted all sizes of organizations, including nonprofits.

Corporate Governance

What is corporate governance supposed to achieve? The corporation, whether for profit or nonprofit, is a separate legal entity whose assets do not belong to any particular constituents. These assets are not the property of those making the decisions. Corporate decisions regarding the use of such assets must be placed in a larger social context. In the United States, the consensus tends to focus on the principal-agent problem and to assume that directors should serve shareholder interests or, in the case of nonprofits, abide by the donor's intent, while producing outcomes for those served. But in other countries, broader social interests are often recognized, and given globalization, these other issues may begin to have an impact in the United States. We assume that widely spread ownership means weak monitoring. However, the mobility of capital in for-profits protects minority shareholders by enabling them to divest easily. This is not the case to the same extent in Europe or Asia. In other countries, organizations have traditionally had large shareholders actively involved in monitoring, so shareholder protection seems less urgent. Although U.S. investors want global convergence based on the U.S. system, they have tended not to recognize that other countries are still concerned with social control. Yet these countries want access to U.S. capital. This tension may not be easy to resolve, yet it holds the key to differing paths of management.

In the nonprofit sector, voluntary board service is also sometimes seen as implying weak monitoring. Although nonprofit board members are usually not paid for their service, they are held to the same levels of responsibility and accountability as paid corporate board members. Hence, nonprofit boards are also being driven to strengthen the independence, reliability, and transparency of their monitoring systems.

Convergence over governance has been occurring in function but not necessarily in form. Many recent studies show that convergence will occur on the U.S.-U.K. pattern. There are significant differences in legal systems, ownership patterns, and social/political systems. But there appears to be some convergence of functions: for example, in transparency, oversight, and an objective audit process. Increasingly, the focus is on substance, not form—specifically, protection of investors, donors, or taxpayers within the context of local traditions. U.S. institutions will continue to play a dominant role in shaping global governance standards.

Accountability and risk management are part of the reason governance has become such a concern. For corporations, several factors raise the requirements for accountability and management of risk. First, foreign direct investment is now much more volatile, and directors must become more aware of ways to minimize the associated risks. Second, corporations throughout the world rely increasingly on global equity financing rather than on bank loans and retained earnings. Third, corporations are increasingly subject to pressures from institutional investors.

What do institutional investors want? What, in short, do corporate and nonprofit investors and citizen taxpayers ultimately seek to achieve by raising governance standards? At heart, they want effective board performance. Having "independent" directors does not necessarily ensure better performance. The OECD principles help to elevate the debate, but they get at only surrogate measures for effective board performance. Patterns of ownership, contributions, taxation, and litigation systems are varied. There is a potential need for the development of a global international standards organization framework for corporate governance. This model set of governance processes could be used as a means for identifying companies with less corporate governance risk. The Conference Board Global Corporate Governance Research Center, its Directors' Institute, and recent blue-ribbon reports are the most significant contributions to this domain and set of issues across all sectors. Many other groups and commentators have articulated recommendations on better governance.

In the nonprofit sector, an emerging issue regarding nonprofit board performance has to do with the ultimate reporting and accountability of nonprofit boards. This question is being raised particularly for foundation boards, but it has implications for nonprofits generally. As argued in the national media, such as the *Chronicle of Philanthropy*, the boards of foundations, as currently organized, are essentially immune to challenge and accountability to any constituency outside the board itself. Of course, the principal accountability of foundations is donor intent, that is, following the intent of the donor who created the foundation. Over time, however, donor intent may be interpreted by foundation boards in ways that would surprise the founder. In some cases, donor intent no longer even makes sense as a guideline, as in the case of foundations set up to care for the veterans of the Civil War or the now famous court decision to go against the explicit intent of the Barnes estate by moving the Barnes collection from the donor's home to a new museum in Pittsburg because this was deemed the only financially viable way to continue to maintain the collection.

But beyond donor intent, how are foundation boards held accountable for the quality of their performance? Corporate boards may be challenged by shareholders if they feel that their financial and social interests are not being served. But currently, foundations and nonprofits have no comparable stakeholder who can formally challenge nonprofit board members over performance. This raises serious challenges that will probably need to be resolved if the sector is to grow in responsibility and in investments. New government oversight for the sector seems the most likely recourse, but this is rife with potential inefficiencies. Is there another mechanism possible that ties the service outcomes of foundations and nonprofits to its constituencies, beyond the self-perpetuating boards?

In the private sector, the market for corporate control, including mergers, proxy contests, and takeovers, has substantially strengthened the board of directors as an institution, as well as the corporate governance system. The development of laws and standards in connection with the unsolicited tender offer has been the most influential factor in this process, because the threat of an unsolicited tender offer keeps boards focused on shareholder value, the role of independent directors, and the role of institutional investors. The judgment of directors is protected by the business-judgment rule. However, a tender offer changes the rules because directors have potential conflicts. Different states have different approaches to this problem. Pennsylvania law, for instance, protects the board at all costs, but this approach may actually weaken the board in relation to management, since management, in effect, can ignore shareholder value. A number of corporations have opted out of the Pennsylvania law.

Delaware, which is the most important corporate state, has a different approach. Under a number of takeover cases, Delaware courts have developed a structure of rules midway between the business-judgment rule and the "entire fairness" test, which traditionally applied when the board was conflicted. This intermediate standard of review is a "reasonably related," or proportionality, test; is there a threat here to corporate policy, and is the response reasonable? The key role must be played by independent directors. Were they informed? Did they have independent advisors? Were they independent of management? This standard of review underscores the role of the board over management. But other cases indicate that the board can pursue a strategy not favored by a majority of the shareholders.

Similar types of conflicts are present in mergers. For example, once the company is for sale, the directors must seek the highest price reasonably available. It should be emphasized that there is continuing and intense competition in the market for corporate control, which puts major responsibilities on the board.

There is a potential lesson in this for the nonprofit sector. Could a version of mergers and acquisitions be designed that would enable effective boards to merge with or acquire other foundations and nonprofits? The nonprofit sector is notorious for the multiplication of organizations and duplications of services. Innumerable organizations approach literacy, for example, with different strategies and methods. No approach is permitted to go to scale, in such an environment, and so the problem persists with multiple, small- to moderate-sized approaches tilting at the dragon. Pride of authorship also prevents the less-effective approaches from acceding to the better-researched and delivered approaches, thus creating ineffectiveness. Safeguards would have to be put in place to maintain donor intent and to prevent dislodging foundations and nonprofits from their local or region-al homes. It would be unfair, for instance, for states with tradi-tionally large and powerful foundations and nonprofits to acquire all the choice foundations and nonprofits around the country. The challenges should not be underestimated. At the same time, a limited merger-and-acquisition approach would introduce a mechanism for giving meaning to nonprofit board performance and would provide them with a competitive meas-ure.

There is a strong movement from inside boards toward more independent directors. Thirty-five years ago, all or mostly inside boards were considered good practice. In the 1970s, to satisfy New York Stock Exchange requirements, companies began to move in the direction of more outside directors. But there was no definition of "independent." The development of the market for corporate control accelerated this trend, as did pressure from institutional shareholders. In addition, the General Motors cor-porate governance principles were issued: the first public statement of how boards should be structured. Another major step was the proposal that the jobs of CEO and chairman be separated, although this has not been followed generally in the United States. Some companies have a "lead director"; however, others, such as Pfizer, use committee chairs to perform this role in their particular areas. For the audit committee, the definition of "independent" has been recently strengthened. Having a majority of independent directors is now standard in the United States. However, many high-tech companies start with largely inside boards, believing that insiders understand the business better. But this typically changes at the time of the initial public offering.

Humanities councils have also tended to have insider boards comprised largely of humanities scholars and university administrators, as mentioned earlier. The parallel case with emerging high-tech companies helps to demonstrate that this is an early-stage structure that may have been suitable when councils were first created more than thirty years ago, but it is not a structure suited to a mature organization, especially in these days of increased governance concerns. To govern a substantive nonprofit, the expertise needed, like that of a corporation, must come from several areas and from a clearly independent set of directors. This includes financial expertise, strategic planning and business modeling, marketing and communications, technology, investment, and experience in senior governance positions. Content expertise in the humanities relates more directly to program content and design rather than to corporate governance and policy. Indeed, few humanities scholars today have either interest or experience in corporate governance and finance. Their expertise lies with disciplinary knowledge that needs to be applied to programming.

When things are going well, less attention is sometimes paid to corporate governance. Differences in corporate governance practices in various countries can be attributed in part to different ownership patterns. For example, in Germany, most major companies have historically been family owned. This is also true in Asia. In Japan, cross-shareholdings are important. This is troublesome for transparency and for corporate governance, but the situation is improving. The role of banks is much more important elsewhere than in the United States. Germany has traditionally been averse to equities, although this is now changing. The Asian capital crisis stimulated a movement toward increased transparency as a means for attracting capital. In many countries, there is major demographic pressure due to aging populations. This has focused attention on developing individual savings through pension plans, which will include equities. This will put more money in institutional hands and increase the demand for shareholder wealth enhancement. The institutions insist on more transparency and better accounting. Issues of the shareholders versus "other constituencies" have recently assumed prominence. Labor mobility is lacking in many countries, compared to that in the United States, and the "social contract" is deemed more important.

Several areas of emphasis will be increasingly important. (1) Companies need a more multicultural human resources policy. (2) Increased transparency of all corporate information will be increasingly urgent. (3) There will be a convergence toward international accounting standards. In addition, issues involving health and labor standards and similar governance issues will also become more important. (4) Many companies are making big bets on information technologies (boards will have to pay more attention to this and the associated costs). (5) Environmental issues—for example, biotech issues and environmental liabilities—will also become more important. In the future, boards will also have to pay closer attention to these issues.

The proliferation of corporate governance codes around the world is uncontestable. This movement has been driven by the relationship between corporate governance and access to capital. The publication of the American Law Institute's *Principles of Corporate Governance* was followed by statements of principles, or guidelines, in a number of other countries. To date, there have been at least seventy guidelines in more than twenty-five countries. These are sometimes linked to stock-exchange disclosure requirements, as in the United Kingdom. There are clear trends in these guidelines. First, most of the guidelines say that the duty of the board is to represent shareholder interests. Second, guidelines usually recognize shareholder interests as a component of maximizing long-term shareholder value. The Vienot Report (France) is somewhat different in emphasizing corporate rather than shareholder interests. But generally speaking, we are seeing a convergence, at least in terms of guideline rhetoric. Third, there is increased emphasis on the board's role in monitoring management and on board objectivity and independent directors. Although these overall trends are clear, the social and legal context is still important to bear in mind. The United States relies much more on independent directors than other countries do and emphasizes stock ownership by directors. We also focus on takeovers more than others do. Because of these differences, it is debatable whether there will ever be a single set of global guidelines.

The perspective of institutional investors has been most powerful in the debate over corporate governance. For instance, TIAA-CREF, the large teacher pension fund, publishes its own statements on corporate governance issues. In many countries, TIAA-CREF has felt that as a minority shareholder, it was being taken advantage of: for example, disparate voting rights and the ability of the majority shareholder to capture assets. TIAA-CREF focused on Europe first and tried to spread its message regarding investor interests. It has conferred with local shareholder groups and many fund managers. Other institutional investors have similar interests. TIAA-CREF now looks at and treats Europe as a single market. The role of pension funds in forcing changes in corporate governance and transparency is becoming increasingly powerful as an impetus to change.

Developments in Japan have not moved as quickly. In the 1980s, the corporate picture in Japan featured large boards with only inside directors; two- to three-year terms of CEOs, no labor market for senior executives, no stock options or other performance incentives, a limited takeover market, and *keiretsu* (a network of interlocking business ownerships and relationships with substantial cross-shareholdings). Now, boards are becoming smaller, with some outside directors; stock options are being introduced but still are not widely used; some companies are now listed on the New York Stock Exchange; and bank loans and main banks are losing their dominant role in corporate finance. With respect to the overall political economy, there is a change away from ministerial guidance to industry self-regulation through trade associations.

Developing countries, primarily in Latin America, have become aware of the need for better corporate governance. The International Finance Corporation promotes private-sector investment in developing countries, invests directly in companies, and acts in an advisory role in, for example, promoting legal and regulatory regimes for capital markets. In Latin America, there has been a large inflow of investment into a relatively small number of companies, and there is a modest potential for convergence in accounting and transparency standards. Generally, Latin America follows the European social and economic model rather than the U.S. model. Family groups have been dominant in corporations in the past. The IFC has been trying to increase director responsibility. Major issues are arising in several areas: the use of nonvoting shares, the role of pension funds in imposing corporate discipline, treatment of minority shareholders, and review and auditing functions. Governments need to address the monitoring of banks and other financial institutions. Investors, hurt in the past, are exercising selectivity and vigilance in all developing countries.

The evolving duties and liabilities of directors are moving in the direction of greater responsibility. The sources of these duties are threefold: statutory duties, the governing instruments of the corporation (charter and by-laws), and judge-made law. The third is the source of fiduciary duties of directors. Directors are fiduciaries because they are handling other people's money. The purpose of establishing fiduciary duties is to ensure the performance of directors' duty to the shareholders. These are the duties of care, loyalty, and good faith. The duty of care requires directors to use all material information reasonably available in making a decision. It regulates procedures, not the substance of decisions. Another aspect of the duty of care is the duty of oversight. The duty of loyalty means that directors must put the interests of shareholders and the corporation ahead of their own interests. The duty of good faith requires directors to act in accordance with law and to try to act in the best interest of the corporation. How are these duties enforced? In the United States, they are enforced mainly by litigation. We make it relatively easy for shareholders to sue. However, there are ways to limit directors' liability. In Delaware, the charter can limit or eliminate liability for violations of the duty of care but not violations of the duty of loyalty. Other states also permit limitation of liability charter provisions. In addition, indemnification by the corporation and liability insurance are available to protect directors. There are also judge-made limitations, such as the business-judgment rule.

The question of what constitutes accountability and to whom directors are accountable is quite apparent. There is, needless to say, a new atmosphere of accountability. Codes are developing, but there probably will not be a standard international code. Most observers are looking at how the market is driving corporate governance. What are the preferences of the market? What is the role of rating agencies and independent researchers? First, boards are being forced to become more accountable to shareholders. This has not been the case in many countries until fairly recently. Accountability to shareholders is taken for granted in Anglo-Saxon systems but not necessarily elsewhere. For example, the two-tier German board is accountable to both labor and shareholders. Second, directors are increasingly required to spend more time on board responsibilities. Third, boards are becoming more independent. Fourth, "stakeholder" issues are becoming a central focus for boards of directors. Fifth, boards are getting a shorter leash. More oversight is seen as necessary.

The need for investors, donors, and taxpayers to look at transparency and governance issues before investing is clear. Good governance is becoming a significant factor today in making investment and charitable decisions. Except in highly publicized cases of dysfunctional boards or fraud, corporate governance practices now receive scrutiny, not after prolonged evidence of bad performance. In fact, there is a debate over the economic value of corporate governance. If society wants companies to have good corporate governance, it has to agree on what information is really needed. Measuring good performance means, among other things, doing a CEO performance review, the board's evaluation of its own performance, and an outside checkup by an independent party. Other, similar measures and systems are needed for nonprofits and government.

There are significant differences between the U.S. and the European liability systems. It appears that the Continental model is moving at least to some extent in the direction of the Anglo-Saxon model. One question is whether the legal liability system will also evolve in a similar direction. It would be logical to argue that there will be some such evolution, on the basis that, if Continental shareholders are demanding new rights, they will also demand new remedies. In the United States, aggrieved shareholders may file class and derivative actions against directors, alleging fraud and mismanagement. The class action is for the most part a uniquely American institution. Prevention of executive misconduct in Europe is accomplished principally by government regulation and criminal sanctions. Two features make class actions much more likely to be brought in the United States than in other countries. The first is the widespread practice of bringing such cases on a contingency basis. The second is the fact that the plaintiff's attorney, upon winning the case or achieving a settlement, is entitled to an award of counsel fees based on a substantial percentage of the amount of the recovery. In general, the culture in European countries, including the United Kingdom, is much less oriented toward litigation.

In takeover battles, for example, litigation in the United States over alleged fiduciary misconduct is very common but in Europe is quite rare. Nevertheless, directors of European companies are by no means free from the risk of lawsuits. This is especially true in the event of insolvency, when receivers or liquidators may bring actions alleging that the negligence of directors contributed to the company's demise or if creditors were misled as to the company's solvency. In France, there is also an action for "abuse of corporate assets" under French law, generally used in cases of self-dealing or excessive remuneration, which may trigger criminal sanctions. Administrative proceedings may also be brought against directors for insider trading and dissemination of false information to the public. A number of such proceedings have been brought by the French Commission des Operations de Bourse. Potential exposure of German directors for claims of mismanagement has led to an increased demand for directors' and officers' liability insurance there.

In European countries, directors are subject to criminal liability in more situations than are U.S. directors: for example, breach of health and safety laws, failure to file tax returns, or failure to comply with social security laws. In addition, foreign companies listed on a U.S. stock exchange can be sued in the United States for allegedly false statements made anywhere in the world if the statements would impact a U.S. securities market. Also, directors of U.S. subsidiaries may be subject to the whole panoply of American fiduciary duties and other remedies, including class and derivative actions and employee suits, which are very common in the United States. The legal liability system is, of course, tied closely to the social, political, and cultural structure of a particular society.

There is considerable evidence today that European societies are moving toward a more open, entrepreneurial model that is willing to question inherited structures. That trend is likely to lead to legal systems that are more open to shareholder rights, takeovers, labor mobility, and litigation. Nonprofits and government, too, are moving toward more entrepreneurial models.

How does litigation apply to these sectors in this new atmosphere?

There is also a growing trend toward more indemnification and insurance for directors. This is true regardless of the size of the company and also extends to the nonprofit sector, where thousands of litigation cases on a host of issues proliferate and make boards wary and nervous, as they can in some cases be held individually liable. It is of critical importance to design a program for the protection of directors and officers: to implement procedures to ensure, to the maximum extent practicable, that their personal assets are not in jeopardy as a result of the business decisions they make. In the United States, many states have statutes allowing corporations to limit or eliminate the liability of their directors in connection with certain types of litigation. Two additional components of a program to protect directors and officers are indemnification and insurance. Both vary from country to country.

In the United States, indemnification requires an affirmative finding by disinterested members of the board, independent counsel, or shareholders that the person seeking indemnification acted in good faith and in a manner reasonably believed to be in, or at least not opposed to, the best interests of the corporation. Indemnification is not available under all circumstances. For example, it may not be available in the case of inability or unwillingness to make that determination; liability to the corporation, including derivative actions; in most jurisdictions, settlement of claims by or in the right of the corporation, including derivative actions; adjudicated violation of the U.S. federal securities laws; and insolvency. Indemnification is less common in other countries, except for the United Kingdom, where it is permissible; it may be available to the directors and officers who acted in accordance with a standard different from the prerequisite to indemnification in the United States. In other countries—for example in France—indemnification may not be available. In Germany, there is no indemnification for members of the management board. Indemnification is permissible for officers who are not members of the supervisory or management board—at least for liabilities resulting from ordinary negligence.

There is no European standard for indemnification. Indemnification laws and customs in Europe are not keeping pace with new exposures. What does this mean? If you are a director of a U.S. subsidiary of a foreign multinational (or vice versa), you should try to secure indemnification from the U.S. entity (through by-laws or contract or both) and from the foreign entity, if possible and available. U.S. indemnification is likely to be broadest; foreign indemnification is a backstop. But, as noted, indemnification is an imperfect solution. You also need insurance to cover (1) the gaps in indemnification and (2) the corporation's indemnification obligation.

D&O insurance has been available in the United States since the early 1970s. Its introduction to the rest of the world has been more recent, but it has been around for a decade or more, and there is an active market in Europe (particularly France and Germany), Australia, Israel, and a few other places. In the United Kingdom, there is concern about domestic third-party litigation. On the Continent, the principal concerns are liability from corporate insolvency, criminal liability, and extraterritorial (principally, U.S.) exposure. U.S. exposures probably drive most of the decisions by foreign multinationals to purchase D&O insurance: specifically, securities liability and extraterritorial reach.

In various jurisdictions, other factors may operate: in the United Kingdom, for example, regulatory investigations, employment practices, environmental, criminal (including corporate manslaughter), insolvency, and shareholders. Proposals have been made to permit U.S.-type shareholder derivative actions. In France, insolvency is a major risk. In Germany, 5% of shareholders can require the corporation to sue directors for breach of duty of care, although this is rarely done; and persons responsible for false and misleading statements in a prospectus can be liable to investors. In Japan, there are hundreds of suits against directors pending. Companies with multinational operations are looking for worldwide coverage. If a U.S. insurance contract is used, make sure that it applies under different indemnification regimes and that it takes advantage of coverage enhancements that might be available under a foreign policy issued to cover a U.S.-based multinational's foreign risk.

When it comes to good governance, problems are avoided when directors understand and embrace their responsibility and focus on growing shareholder value. In a recent PricewaterhouseCoopers international study including extensive interviews with directors and corporate governance experts in several countries, new findings emerged. The study found that there were eight major responsibilities of the board: strategy and planning; risk management; ethics and values—the tone at the top; measuring and monitoring company performance; transformational transactions; external communications; management evaluation, compensation, and succession planning; and board operations. Three overall themes emerged: information (getting the right information, especially information on risks), risk management (i.e., a risk- identification process to identify risks), and board dynamics (boards must be actively involved and not simply reactive). CEOs need an active board. If we assume a "board involvement continuum" from "hands off" to "in management's hair," we would avoid either extreme, but today, we should be moving toward the active-involvement end of the continuum.

Numerous shareholder proposals recently submitted to a number of companies are designed to enable shareholders to vote more effectively. Proxy-advisory firms will give advice to institutional shareholders on how to vote their stock. These proposals are somewhat different in that they contemplate that the company itself would hire a proxy-advisory firm to make its advice available to all shareholders. The proxy-advisory firm would be chosen by shareholder vote and would be independent of management. The Internet increases the possibility for information to flow to shareholders.

The process of selecting directors is also changing. Until recently, the process was weak but has recently improved. The Blue Ribbon Committee's conclusions, including the recommendation that audit committee members be financially literate and that more-independent directors be included, are being taken very seriously. They should be in nonprofit boards as well.

Corporate Culture, Civil Society, and Justice

The idea of corporate culture has become central to thought about corporations in today's world. Corporate culture is grounded in the core values and missions of corporations and in increasing accountability and transparency in governance. The idea has become popular as a way to help large companies focus and clarify the core purposes and activities that should guide and connect tactics and action. By highlighting the larger purposes of the corporation, everyone—shareholders, board, executives, and staff—can better understand how their efforts contribute to a larger good and can improve the strategies and tactics to better support the larger purpose. An emphasis on the values and purposes of corporate culture is an early development of a needed, larger articulation of the humanistic and ethical purposes of commerce. Corporate culture also includes the governance of an organization, including the tone and example set by leadership and the commitment to transparency and openness.

At the same time, the phrase *corporate culture* may seem to be an oxymoron. To many, especially those in the cultural sector of society, corporations and culture are like oil and water. Corporations value earnings, efficiency, and utility and follow markets and trends without asking whether the desires represented by such trends are ultimately good or bad. This agnosticism toward the ultimate ends of market activity suggests to many that corporations do not represent a deep culture or possess a deeper connection to culture and its values. Culture, by contrast, values knowledge and service over earnings as intrinsic goods, inefficiencies (e.g., taking more time than is "necessary" to view a painting) and meaning over utility, and consciously resists market forces, trends, and fads in the name of higher, intrinsic knowledge and values that have stood the tests of time. This difference of perspective, further, tends to set up culture as a higher judge of corporations, corporate culture, and the effects of corporate activity on society and the environment. Hence, within modern culture, there is a built-in contrarian attitude and critical stance on the part of culture with respect to corporations.

The roots of this opposition between culture and corporations are firmly grounded in modern philosophy's bifurcation of the world into science/technology and culture, facts and feelings, and practice and imagination, with higher value given to the side of culture, imagination, and feeling. Ultimately, Descartes' division of the world into the *res extensa* (the physical world) and the *res cogitans* (the mental world) undergirds this division, although Descartes did not attribute higher status and value to *res cogitans*; that development came later through German Idealism and Romanticism. This dualism came to be taken at face value as common sense, so much so that the 1795 edition of the *Encyclopedia Britannica* concluded its definition of *philosophy* by declaring the idea to be definitive and unquestionable, with this final paragraph:

> Philosophy singles out the characteristic phenomena which distinguish every substance; and philosophy will never hesitate in saying that there is a set of phenomena which characterize mind and another which characterize body, and that these are toto coelo different. Continually appealing to fact, to the phenomena, for our knowledge of every cause, we shall have no difficulty in deciding that thought, memory, volition, joy, hope are not compatible attributes with bulk, weight, elasticity, fluidity.[2]

This ontological division served as the gold reserve to guarantee the broader social application of this division of labor and value. Thus, over time, the defining features of humanity were clustered around imagination, emotion, and cultural enrichment, whereas the activities tied to practical affairs were devalued. In one of Van Gogh's landscapes, this thought is presented visually by dividing the painting between a path leading through a healthy landscape to a church on the horizon on the right and a path leading through a blighted wasteland to a factory on the horizon to the left.

As illustrated in that painting, the human world of value and the corporate worlds of work and everyday life exist at the ends of separate paths, inhabiting totally separate compartments. The point is made even more bluntly by French writer Montaigne:

> We should set aside a back-room [*une arriereboutique*] reserved exclusively to ourselves, keeping it entirely free, and establishing therein our true liberty, our principal retreat and solitude. There our normal discourse should be with, addressed to ourselves, so privy that no contact or communication with the outside can find a place there. We should converse and laugh as though we had no wife or children, no possessions, no followers, no servants.... We have a soul which can turn inward on itself; able to keep itself company; capable of attack and defense, of reception and donation. Let us have no fear of decaying in that solitude through idle boredom.[3]

Following Montaigne, modern culture has created itself in the form of an *arriereboutique*, a private backroom where we are invited to indulge our totally private reflections on ourselves. Note also Montaigne's identification of this separate cultural space as "true liberty," and contrast that with models that define liberty in social differentiation and action. Here, in the realm of culture, we are invited to separate ourselves from the daily affairs of family life, commerce, and social duties and relations and to live in solipsistic bliss, a complete world unto ourselves. Stated so graphically and emphatically, it can be seen that the claims of modern culture to privileged status are really shocking and extreme. Such a viewpoint, however, continues to set the world of daily life and commerce apart from human experience and value, however ill-advisedly.

Today, the philosophical and ontological arguments for this bifurcation have collapsed. There is no broad philosophical or scientific consensus for this view, but the broad attitude about culture and practical affairs remains with us as a kind of echo, or residue. With no strong philosophical basis to back it up, and with the new forces at work today, it is time to acknowledge that this perspective is counterproductive. Today, the tension between culture and corporate organization is an anachronism and an obstacle to enlarging human experience and value.

If the Cartesian and romantic residue were swept away, it is possible to see the outlines of a deeper connection between corporations and humane culture. How does the structure of corporations relate to civil society? Are justice and human happiness furthered by corporate organization? What is the connection, if any, between justice and a society organized in large measure through corporations?

At heart, corporations are voluntary organizations. The term *voluntary organization* is usually reserved for the nonprofit sector, but this is an inaccurate way to distinguish the sectors. Corporations share with nonprofits, as opposed to government, the quality of voluntary association and participation. In a free society, it makes sense for most of the activity of society to be organized in this way. Through corporate charters and organizations, individuals voluntarily come together to organize their efforts toward some goal or end. In the business sector, this voluntary association is intended to produce mutual benefit, as well as to meet the demands and needs of customers. In the nonprofit sector, voluntary association is designed to be independent of the mutual benefit of the corporation's members. Independence from direct benefit is intended to help the boards of nonprofits to serve the broader community and long-term goals. (Whether or not this is the result of independence is an interesting question.)

If civil society is understood as arising from the voluntary association of the members of society, it can be seen that corporations and nonprofits both contribute to, or better yet, constitute, the fabric of civil society. A single emphasis on the third sector as the basis of civil society sets the focus too narrowly and leaves out social, organizational, and economic dynamics that are critical to the existence of civil society. This is a lesson worth remembering as others seek to replicate or build civil society around the world. This would suggest that active support of corporations is intrinsic to civil society. Corporations are not aberrations allowed by civil society; they are part of the genetic code of civil society.

Thus, there is a continuum of shared values between corporations and civil society, not a gap between two different, incompatible value systems.

Further, corporate structure is designed to facilitate and enable differentiation of knowledge and work. In the industrial era, with its mindless division of labor and crude integration of machinery and people, differentiation came to be seen as a form of dehumanization and alienation. Karl Marx was one of the major figures to articulate this point of view. The shortcomings of industrialism, however, are tied more to the primitive means for combining human and technical interactions and a failure to connect tasks with mission, vision, and governance in a coherent manner.

Again, when those issues are clarified and distinguished from organizational issues, a connection between justice and social differentiation can become clear. As suggested earlier, a just society supports each individual's well-being (i.e., optimal integration and self-expression—*autow pratein*, to use the Greek term from Plato—or pursuit of happiness, to use the founders' phrase), while ensuring that that individual pursuit is compatible with the pursuits of others. Put another way, a just society is highly differentiated. A just society is a "coat of many colors" that displays the scope of human interests and character in a well-adapted social fabric that organizes and sustains such diversity.

Diversity here goes deeper than multiculturalism, because it is grounded in active human drives and aspirations rather than in historical artifacts and past identities. This also explains why, when given the choice, people tend to choose the active drive rather than historical identity. Of course, this tendency runs counter to the traditional ideas about the higher value of culture described earlier. If all deeply human qualities are defined in culture, people who choose products and services produced through corporate activity must be acting against their well-being and happiness. Such choices can be explained only as some type of illusion created by advertising and marketing, in the old view. If the modern assumption about the separate and superior status of culture is ill-founded, as noted earlier, the idea that cultural identity trumps all forms of identity collapses.

From a more practical, less philosophical perspective, one can also question the legitimacy of the old modern view of culture in the following way. Are cultures static structures? Isn't the meaning of a culture or cultural practice dependent upon how we choose to develop it? If human beings are free to choose how to interpret their experience, does this not also apply to cultural inheritance? Perhaps the belief that people are nothing but the products of their culture and that people become alienated when they diverge from their culture reflects not a truth about culture but a choice that has been made by those who fear the responsibility of making autonomous choices required by the active drive. Is the choice of historical identity just that, a choice? Can it sometimes be a pathological choice?

On the other hand, if a just society is highly diverse and diversified, it is reasonable to expect a bewildering array of choices expressed, from the ridiculous to the sublime. The justice of such a system is that it enables such diversity—such "plentitude," as Leibniz would put it—not that it conforms to a predefined set of outcomes that fall under a separate value rubric, such as a separate set of cultural values. As Virginia Wolfe once said, "nothing human shocks me." The humane insight of that statement should be embraced when observing economic behavior.

In sum, by laying aside anachronistic cultural ideas, it can be seen that civil society is continuous with corporate organization; in fact, civil society is defined by corporate organization: some for profit, some nonprofit. Further, if justice is optimal personal and social integrity and self-expression, corporate organization is a critical means for achieving personal as well as social justice. The well-integrated character that we have defined as both "just" and "happy" is replicated in the well-adapted society. This suggests another reason why character is critical to capitalism and why civil society is critical to corporations.

Realigning our ideas about corporate culture with civil society and justice, as briefly sketched here, would require adjustments in thinking on both sides. From the cultural sector, made up largely of academic, cultural, and religious institutions, this would mean acknowledgment that they share a common set of values and social space with corporations—they do not represent a distinct, more humane, and per se higher set of values. The sector shares a common humanity with the corporate sector. On the side of business corporations, this also means that more attention needs to be paid to human happiness and the aims of a full human life as a part of corporate responsibility. Some activities are undertaken because of their intrinsic value, not because they are useful to some other purpose. If care for this dimension of human life cannot be relegated to a separate cultural sphere, it must help inform the "culture" of business corporations. This change is already under way in corporations, as recent business practice has begun to focus more on mission, values, and corporate responsibility.

There are seemingly endless issues of corporate responsibility. The three primary issues of responsibility are economic, social, and environmental. Companies today need to focus on wider analysis, particularly if they go into less-developed markets. This is sometimes called "reputation management." There are no firm, agreed-upon standards and no reporting standards for such issues. Therefore, companies have to be creative. One possible alternative is to establish a committee on global integrity and accountability. Royal Dutch Shell, for example, issues a "sustainability report," and other companies are moving in a similar direction. Nonprofits have long placed a high value on the substance of their missions and the ethical standards of their practices, which are seen as implementation of the human values they serve. Taking a page from the corporate experience, nonprofits today might well create their own committees to define and publish their organizations' positions on corporate integrity and accountability.

As human and social capital become increasingly critical to corporate success, a corporate responsibility to nurture the pursuit of happiness and civility will need to take shape. As many companies have learned, creative, highly motivated individuals will leave good positions if their human needs are not being met. Likewise, if the community around an enterprise does not offer the cultural and educational resources creative people need, they will go elsewhere. Self-interest, if nothing larger, would suggest that corporate responsibility must address these areas in the future, thus putting corporations into activities once reserved for cultural and educational corporations.

The future of democracy and civil society depends to a far greater extent than we might have thought in the past on the success of corporations as key structures through which people freely associate and work together in a highly diversified society. Companies—large, small, public, private, and social— depend on sound governance and the flow of and access to information and financial resources. Corporations cannot survive in simply any kind of society. In the Soviet Union, for example, private corporations were forbidden without special permission. The political and economic environment is critically important to the flourishing of corporations. In most civilized countries, we tend to concentrate on practice and not often enough on ideas. It is clear that socialism as an economic system is over and that capitalism has prevailed, but we have not thought sufficiently about all of the implications of this transition.

Liberty is another instance of the importance of ideas. We should understand that natural liberty includes political liberty and economic liberty of enterprises, as well as moral and cultural liberty, each of which requires personal integrity and character. Governance systems are rooted in both personal liberty— grounded in character and the pursuit of happiness—and public liberty and the good of the commonwealth. Good governance, thus, brings us back again to the importance of personal integrity (happiness), liberty, and life that the founders placed at the center of society and government.

Corporations began as burial societies, then in the Middle Ages transformed into monasteries, towns, and universities. They were legally constituted, independent of the state, transgenerational, and intended to endure. Most corporations began around an idea—an act of creativity. Monasteries, for example, were hotbeds of invention and predecessors of transnational corporations. The development of Western Europe was based on the premise that the Creator gave human beings creative powers (made them in His image); in contrast to other societies, men believed that they could invent without being seen as disturbing the fixed order of the universe. This creative activity rooted in a public philosophy and the rule of law gave raise to evolving standards of corporate governance. The public humanities were critical in framing this development. Unfortunately, the humanities have become too marginalized from the mainstream of economic development and thought in recent decades, thereby failing society and corporations in a time of crisis and opportunity in corporate governance. Can humanities organizations today exemplify themselves with globally competitive governance and transparency in their own operations? Can the humanities rediscover their role in defining governance for today's world and in training a cadre of leaders and students in personal and business ethics and good practice? Our fate and the fate of liberty, happiness, and life lie in the balance.

It has been said that modernity believes in nothing. This state of nothingness—the absence of any sense of truth—leaves a cosmic void. There can be no greatest good, because the highest standing can never exceed one's personal preference or individual values. What Eric Voegelin called "very comfortable nihilism" has come to mean that whatever we want to be true is literally true for us.[4] Such a state of groundlessness becomes not only superficial but also spiritually eroded. We have argued that the renewal of American culture is ultimately dependent on an openness to transcendence. To great extent, civil society is possible only when the *civitas* answers and articulates meaningful answers to the question of civility. Is it too much to think that godliness might again drive us toward a community of shared participation in transcendence? Throughout their long history, Americans have seen themselves as agents of progress and grace in the world. They have achieved what they have as a rational order maximizing individual freedom and earthly happiness. We can renew our culture by again taking up our manifest destiny, not in some physical sense to increase territory but to disseminate a view of human happiness and flourishing so that the entire world will become American through and to the extent that it too participates in perfect liberty.

Notes

1. "Not for Profit Management," *McKinsey Quarterly* (December 14, 2005).
2. "Definition of Philosophy," *Encyclopedia Britannica*, 1795.
3. Michel Montaigne, *Essais: Book One* (London: Athlone Press, 1986), p. xxxix.
4. Eric Voegelin, *The New Science of Politics* (Chicago: University of Chicago Press, 1987).

10

A Bright, Life-Affirming Future

Need for a Grand Narrative

HUMAN BEINGS UNDERSTAND THEMSELVES as temporal beings, with a past, a present, and a future. We tell stories to ourselves and about ourselves as individuals, members of a particular culture or tradition, and members of the human race. Even those who deny the need for such stories—because they believe that sometime in the *future*, we shall have a complete account of all knowledge (scientism)—are forced to give us a story about where we started and how we are progressing to that point. There is no avoiding the creation and endorsement of a narrative—a story line.

These narratives form the basis of social capital, a greater part of which in America is found in spiritual capital. Recent studies show that over one-half of social capital is stored in religious and philosophical voluntary institutions, most not formally tied to an ecclesiastical organization. These places of gathering, of thought and prayer, of assembly, of voluntary activity and charity or social exchange are critical to the longevity and health of our society. Most have their foundation in some form of the public humanities, broadly conceived. When they decline or fail to develop, civil society ceases to exist or fully function.

In longer-term perspective, both historical and philosophical, it is obvious that thinkers from Aquinas to de Tocquiville and from Althusius to Burke have commented on the same phenomenon. Whether it was the "little platoons" that make life possible or the mediating structures of public life, these spheres have in antiquity and in recent times been critical to the health of society and the balancing of interests vis à vis the state.

Moreover, these narratives have a profound effect on action. **There appears too much truth empirically founded in the adage that societies with an abundance of social capital are healthier, more democratic, and more prosperous.** In recent studies, trust, personal networks, and a sense of community have been found to play important parts in thriving organizations. Social capital, it turns out, is so integral to business life that without it, corporate action—and, consequently, productive work—is not possible. Social capital involves the social elements that contribute to knowledge sharing, innovation, and high productivity. It seems apparent that in the same sense, some organizations thrive as a result of their stored social capital, whereas others fail for its lack. If social capital is such a critical factor in the success of organizations and the competitiveness of countries or economic systems, its value must be underscored. It is no surprise, then, that nation building and economic development have become so enamored with notions of social capital.

How we understand the future has a critical effect on how we understand the present and how we act. The stories we tell—the narratives of the future that we create as a culture—set a horizon toward which our actions and thoughts tend and serve as a source for social capital through our religious and philanthropic organizations. Without such a horizon, we feel bewildered and lost. The present is bewildering for many people today because we lack a consensus narrative about the future. Hence, one of the most significant marks of transformation for our society and societies around the globe is a new, integrated, and broadly shared story about our common future, our destiny, and our common-wealth.

Neither the good nor a good life can be reduced to one rule or a set of rules. It is embedded as narrative and example in the lives of real human beings. Without the cultivation of perceptual judgment, without historical insight grounded in the examples of leaders and individuals who exemplify various types of goodness and character, we lose touch with the sustaining truths of life that we need to guide us into the future. For too long, our culture has replaced these personal narratives with exposés based on abstract theories that purport to be universal and "nonanthropocentric." As Charles Taylor points out in *Sources of the Self,* a "nonanthropocentric" ethics and value system is virtually a contradiction in terms.[1] The very core of ethical thinking and judgment is the anthropology of moral life—the narratives of choice, motivation, and nuance and the suitability of an action to its particular situation. The amelioration of moral action depends upon the continuation of this narrative, sustained through moral dialogue, literature, historical study, and religious communities. Surely one of the clear lessons of the twentieth century is that abstract theories of rights, political ideologies, centralized systems designed to deliver moral goods through policy, fiat, and other variations on abstract value systems have not replaced these more vibrant, biographical, community-based narratives of exemplary life and action. What these narratives lack in theoretical clarity and aspiration to universal reforms that sweep away the vagaries of history and precedent, they make up for in the power of example and community to transform lives.

Hannah Arendt wrote in *The Human Condition* about the terror of evil and its banality.[2] She and others since have tried to restore a balance between the *via activa* (the active life) and the *via contemplativa* (the life of the mind). Such a balance is necessary more than ever today. This balancing is the proper and expected role for the public humanities in the early part of the twenty-first century. In a period when shrill voices, demagoguery, mere entertainment, and shallowness have become dominant cultural forces, **there is an urgent cry for humaneness, civility, and a restored sense that human beings and the cultures they form and interact in should be rooted in a theory of development anchored not only in ever-growing material wealth but also a philosophy of human flourishing.**

Practical people may disagree about virtue or which virtues to exalt, but it is the humanities as the keeper of wisdom and personal narrative that allow and encourage such dialogue and contain it in the public sphere. It is rare anywhere this day to hear intelligent people describe or debate what is virtuous. We have virtuous cycles, virtuous or excellent companies, and even the virtuous athletic performance (perfect games). But there is a vacuum left by the diminution of the sacred, the communal, and the personal and little to fill the void.

In this new Internet age and for the foreseeable future, we are bombarded daily with ever more bits and bytes of data that ultimately become fashioned into usable information flows. This information so overloads us today that we seek ever-better and cleaner ways to decipher, protect, store, and retrieve it. At a certain point and with analysis, information streams are shaped into knowledge. We are creating more knowledge than ever before, at a rate that often exceeds our human capacities to comprehend it. More knowledge has been created in the past seven years than all that collected in past history, it is claimed. At some point, we are forced to ask the most critical questions: about truth and justice, about what is good and right, and about beauty itself. What mechanisms, formulas, and means do we have at our disposal to answer such quandaries and ultimate questions? Data, information, and knowledge alone or even together help, but they will not suffice. Couple the avalanche of information with rigid sectarian disputes, and the result is increasing fragmentation. At some point, a broad, inclusive, humane vision is needed: a vision with historical perspective larger than individual perception, a dialogue broader than the familiar talking points of ideology, sect, or peer focus group.

Challenge to the Humanities: Develop Such a Narrative

The Humanities in Times Past

Especially at times of significant cultural change, such as the present, there is a genuine need for a way to create forms of continuity with the wisdom of the past. Writing about the philosophical schools in the imperial Roman period, an earlier period of globalization and cultural clashes, Pierre Hadot outlined the efforts of thinkers of that day to build a substantive and respectful dialogue among the various philosophical, scientific, mathematical, ethical, and religious traditions and currents of the day. As he put it in *What Is Ancient Philosophy*:

> Neoplatonism after Plotinus...might seem at first to be a development of Plotinus' hierarchic system. In fact, however, it is characterized by a gigantic attempt at synthesizing the most disparate elements of the philosophical and religious traditions of all antiquity. In conformance with a long tradition, Platonism was identified with Pythagoreanism. At the same time, Aristotelianism was reconciled with Platonism, insofar as Aristotle's writings, interpreted in a Platonic sense, represented the first stage in the overall cursus of Neoplatonic teaching. This consisted in the explanation of some of Aristotle's treatises, and then of Plato's dialogues, ordered in accordance with the stages of spiritual progress.

> Harmonization did not stop here, however. There was also an attempt to create agreement with the philosophical tradition on the one hand, and on the other with the Orphic writings and the Chaldean Oracles, considered to be traditions revealed by the gods. The task was thus to systematize all revealed doctrines—Orphism, Hermeticism, and Chaldeanism—with the philosophical tradition, whether Pythagorean or Platonic.... [In time this came to include religious rituals] these rituals included ablutions, sacrifices, and invocations using ritual words.... The later Neoplatonists believed that because the soul had fallen into the body, it needed to go through material and sensible rites in order to be able to rise toward the divine. This was similar to the move made by Christianity, in which man, once corrupted by original sin, needs the mediation of the incarnate Logos and the sensible signs of the sacraments.[3]

Compare this intellectual spirit of inclusion, respect, and higher-order synthesis with the "winner-take-all" tenor of debates among political, religious, secular, scientific, artistic, and academic protagonists today.

The Present State of the Humanities

Symptomatic of the present state of the humanities is a willful devaluing of the past. We see the modern spirit expressed by Descartes, to wipe the slate clean, to explicitly reject history and personal biography as sources of knowledge, and to try to generate a universal system out of whole cloth. The result is a form of intellectual and moral rigidity that is strikingly at odds with the open and respectful intellectual culture described by Hadot. Could one imagine today a deeply respectful, productive discussion among a devout Muslim, a secularist, an evangelical Christian, a liberal Democrat, an astrophysicist, a devout Jew, a genetic biologist, a conservative Republican, a Hollywood producer, a Hindu, a mathematician, an artist, and a humanist? Could such a group today even manage the first step of listening to one another deeply, much less move on to create some genuine common ground? If such a conversation is not even conceivable, how can we expect to have the broad, integrative wisdom to guide globalization along peaceful and productive paths?

The present state of the humanities is also characterized by an extreme methodological rigor rooted in early modern thinkers in France. In his chapter "How the French Wanted Reforms Before They Wanted Freedom," Alexis de Tocqueville described the views of early social reformers in France more than a century before the French Revolution. For these reformers, according to de Tocqueville:

> The past was an object of limitless contempt. "The nation has been governed by false principles for centuries; everything seems to have been done at random," says Letrone. Starting from this idea, they set to work; there was no institution too old, too well-founded, for them not to demand its abolition, because it was inconvenient to them and disturbed the symmetry of their plans.... Thus it was not a question of destroying absolute

power but of converting it… "The state makes men whatever it wants," says Bodeau. This phrase sums up all their theories.

This immense social power that the [reformers] imagined was not only greater than any of the powers which they could see around them; it differed from them in its origin and character too. It did not derive directly from God; it was not at all attached to tradition; it was impersonal: it was no longer called the king, but the state; it was not the inheritance of a family; it was the product and the representative of everyone, and must make the rights of each bend before the will of all.[4]

Critics will no doubt point out that we live in an age of multiple and competing narratives. This is what it means to live in the *postmodern world*. Moreover, when faced with competing narratives, the various protagonists have engaged in unprecedented forms of character assassination and delegitimation. The delegitimators have in turn been delegitimated themselves. There is no narrative on which all will agree and no way, given the limitations of discursive thought, to persuade everyone to accept the same narrative. So where does that leave us?

Our response is that this is precisely what the founders understood when they proclaimed and endorsed the pursuit of happiness. To endorse the pursuit of happiness is to endorse the recognition that different individuals have different substantive views of human fulfillment. Unable to agree on abiding substantive norms, we can nevertheless agree on procedural norms. One of our procedures is precisely on how to agree to disagree! The founders were able to achieve this insight because they subscribed to personal narratives that embodied substantive norms that permitted them to deal with the fact that others did not share the same narrative. One of the great strengths of the Judeo-Christian heritage, as Locke pointed out in his essay "Toleration," is that it made room for tolerance.[5] In short, the founders found the resources within their personal narratives to tolerate alternative views.

What the Declaration of Independence produced was a meta-narrative that recognized, encompassed, and tolerated alternative narratives. It recognized that our tradition, or inheritance, contained divergent voices, but it found a way of encompassing those voices rather than excluding or delegitimating them. The unwillingness or inability to offer a metanarrative that encompasses differences reflects the unwillingness or inability to think through one's own position, the incapacity of one's narrative to encompass differences, or perhaps a refusal to lay one's cards on the table. To refuse to do so is, in the end, not to be able to understand the position of others who do offer a full articulation of their position and therefore incapacitates one for reaching a meaningful resolution.

In the world of biology, a new question has arisen. Stated elegantly in Simon Conway Morris's work, especially in *Life's Solution: Inevitable Humans in a Lonely Universe*, Morris suggests that evolution has a purpose, an overall structure.[6] Not only does life have an uncanny knack of navigating to precise solutions, but also it repeatedly returns to similar solutions. Scientists have been proving the ubiquity of evolutionary convergence, which unexpectedly reveals a deeper structure to life. One finding in the tape of life is that to date, underpinned by DNA and guided by a genetic code of staggering effectiveness, only humans have been able to navigate such properties as advanced sensory systems, intelligence, complex societies, tool making, and culture. We have no counterparts here or on other planets. We are, inevitably humans, yes, but in a lonely universe.

At some point and somehow, is it not unreasonable to note that evolution has produced us as a species with this sense of purpose. Life on Earth is still surrounded with improbabilities, as well as endless opportunities for the common good and the enrichment of us all. C. K. Chesterton said: "The most brilliant exponent of the egoistic school, Nietzsche, with deadly and honorable logic, admitted that the philosophy of self-satisfaction led to looking down upon the weak, the cowardly, and the ignorant."[7] In today's upside-down world, it is, strangely, the victims who have come to be self-satisfied in their perennial weakness and a state of mind and being that masks anger as political correctness, thereby incapacitating true action and generational progress. Are we all really victims? Is that the last word?

Future of the Humanities

The humanities as collectors of stored wisdom from the sages of human experience, as progenitors of values and values-based education, are a central component of social capital. In fact, it could be argued that they are the critical link between past wisdom and the future on the shared values that make human existence more than possible, even heroic. **If the humanities are to flourish and regain their rightful place in public life—if they are to influence public discourse for the good—they must be based in a philosophy of the pursuit of happiness.** Doing so, they must affirm life. The affirmation of life is as old as thought itself and is tied to the wisdom of every tradition that has had any lasting influence in human progress across civilizations. Those modes of thought are philosophic, religious, and scientific. There is no Cartesian divide when it comes to the notion that human life is worthy and dignified. Throughout the centuries and in myriad ways, rulers, priests, kings, judges, and teachers from around the world have held up human life as a central answer to the very question of being. In the past century, wars and cynical ideologies sought to replace notions of the common good and human flourishing with cults of personality, ideologies of totalitarianism, and praises of death and violence. This complete surrender to evil culminated in numerous holocausts, suffering on an unprecedented scale, and near utter philosophical despair.

Virtue must be founded on something; it is not relative or subjective. Like the arc and circumference of a circle, virtue refers to some point outside itself. Historically, some concept of transcendence has been the fulcrum for the development of virtues that in past eras have sustained human flourishing. Can it do so again? In the twelfth-century Duomo in Florence, there is a profoundly visual depiction of virtue. Following an iconographic program inspired by prevailing Scholastic thought, the hexagonal reliefs represent the human activities related to the virtues of *necessitas* (civil life, supreme sciences, intellectual speculation); the mythical inventions of the arts (painting, sculpture, and architecture); liberal arts, grammar, dialectic, rhetoric and arithmetic, medicine, geometry and astronomy; the divine virtues (faith, hope, and charity); and the cardinal virtues (wisdom, justice, temperance, and courage). The twenty-first century is not likely to build new cathedrals or to fully embrace the ancients. But one has to ask whether it would not make sense for the humanities, particularly in their public face, to reestablish themselves on the basis of a serious discussion of virtues: past, present, and future.

A crucial element in the metanarrative of the Declaration was the recognition of personal autonomy. Doctrines, religious or otherwise, have no meaning unless freely and willingly embraced by individuals who understand what they mean. This respect for human autonomy was rooted in the relationship to transcendence. To offer a metanarrative that does not focus on autonomy would be to misunderstand both ourselves and the world we presently live in; to offer a metanarrative that contravenes autonomy is to flirt with threats to liberty.

It is the humanities that have often best articulated this vision and helped to defend its status. An enlightened public, religiously alert, grounded in the classics, and realizing the treasure of liberty stored in the humanities, is the bedrock of human and social capital. The humanities must continue to uphold this tradition and to educate a widening public, now global in nature, to the benefits and consequences of learning and practicing spiritual capital formation. The real mark of transformation for the public humanities as a whole—broadly defined as endowments, universities, cultural institutions, and humanities councils and their constituents—is how well they are building up a stock of spiritual, human, and social capital.

More than ever in a global, complex, and technological setting, and on a lonely planet, we seek wisdom, a dialogue grounded in the good that the humanities were created to foster and to sustain. The humanities are a critical source of

human and social capital, a wellspring of civic-mindedness, and essential to democracy and civil life. We will know that they are achieving their intended purpose when they help to build more and lasting social capital. Out of such a constructive dialogue, a new, humane vision can grow, linking the spiritual and the economic, the scientific and the religious, leadership with service, globalization with localization, the vast new vision of the cosmos with the humane vision of life, liberty, and above all, the pursuit of happiness.

Notes

1. Charles Taylor, *Sources of the Self: The Making of the Modern Identity* (Cambridge, MA: Harvard University Press, 1989).
2. Hannah Arendt, *The Human Condition* (Chicago: University of Chicago Press, 1998).
3. Pierre Hadot, *What Is Ancient Philosophy?* (Cambridge, MA: Harvard University Press, 2002), pp. 168–169, 171.
4. Alexis de Tocqueville, "How the French Wanted Reforms Before They Wanted Freedom," in A. S. Kahan, trans., *Democracy in America* (Chicago: University of Chicago Press, 1998), pp. 210–212.
5. John Locke, *Two Treatises on Government and a Letter Concerning Toleration* (New Haven, CT: Yale University Press, 2003).
6. Simon Conway Morris, *Life's Solution* (Cambridge: Cambridge University Press, 2003).
7. C. K. Chesterton, *Orthodoxy*, reprint edition (New York: Ignatius Press, 1995), p. 132.

Appendix
Thirty-Six Propositions

W E ALL HAVE to-do lists, action lists, shopping lists, and lists for this and that. Whether it is Ten Commandments, seven habits, or nine suggestions, people have been making lists to keep score or to form culture since time immemorial. Some lists, nailed to cathedral doors in the form of Luther's Ninety-Five Theses, actually changed history.

In the mid-1980s, Peter Berger, the renowned sociologist, took on the Marxists and provided a tough-minded, provocative analysis of how capitalism, as the great engine of change, had revolutionized modern life. His empirical findings laid a basis for a powerful and testable new theory to shape what he termed "economic culture." The core idea was simply that the modern market economy we call capitalism transforms every other aspect of society. In his final chapter, Berger postulated "Fifty Propositions" about prosperity, equality, and liberty. The purpose of the stated propositions was "to take a look at these propositions as a whole and then to ask what practical uses emergent theory may have."

In a similar vein but not so narrowly focused on economics, we have forged a large argument, a case, about the vast, tectonic changes under way and the opportunity to renew American culture and global transformation through the "pursuit of happiness." Not everyone will read our philosophical and detailed treatment and all its caveats, nuances, and tensions. Some will focus on the economic thesis; others will applaud that religion is again taken seriously; still others will deeply appreciate the cultural impact we have outlined and the importance of the humanities and will find it hopeful. But for those who want or need a neater summary treatment and for those who go to the end first, here are *Thirty-Six Propositions* that, taken together, could do nothing less than bring about a renewal of American culture.

We want to address these propositions to a new generation— a generation of leaders only now coming of age—and to their successors. Although we appreciate the interest and engagement of leaders currently at work, many of whom are contributing to the vast change under way, we believe that it is the next, succeeding generations that will truly grasp the meaning of these changes and shape them into a new culture.

We call to a rising generation of humanist leaders in business, government, education, and the nonprofit sectors to forge a new integration of global commerce, learning, technology, service, and a global rule of law into a new culture grounded in the pursuit of happiness. This is the work of a new generation because the scope of the change is so great.

So, to those generations now rising, whose members have always known the Internet, global communications, new economies, and vastly expanded capacities to learn and create, we make our case and issue a challenge. To these generations, it is as if they are given the opportunity to be present for the birth of language, the invention of the printing press, and the start of the Renaissance all at once. That is, these generations have the opportunity to work with truly new systems of code and meaning; new, smart technologies for communicating; and opportunities for the most creative minds around the world to inspire one another to create new works from these new systems and knowledge. We sound a trumpet call to these young leaders to rise to the creative potential before them, and we suggest the following to guide their work. (The pages on which these propositions are stated and explored are noted in parentheses after each proposition).

The Propositions for Renewing American Culture

1 THE PURSUIT of happiness is a uniquely American dynamic and outlook that continues to shape our destiny and now affects people around the world. (p. 2)

2 THIS TRANSCENDENT RIGHT is not derived from any government, institution, or individual and is unalienable. (p. 6)

3 IT FOLLOWS THAT the central purpose of government, culture, and work is to put power in the service of human flourishing. (p. 6)

4 THE FOUNDERS' bold wager that the purpose of society is supporting each individual's definitive right to live freely and happily is the most monumental experiment in history. (p. 9)

5 THE RAPID, INTERLINKED DYNAMICS of technology, the growth of knowledge, and globalization have created a perfect storm of change—all unleashed by the American experiment. (pp. 18 and 43)

6 THE OLD, TRADITIONAL GULF between the spiritual and the economic can be bridged because economic activity has a spiritual basis: a "spiritual form of capital" that is linked to human and social capital. (p. 21)

7 GENUINE ECONOMIC GROWTH is creative management of endowed resources by stewards acting on their commitments, guided by normative laws, character, and principled habits and practices. (p. 27)

8 THE OVERRIDING MORAL QUESTION of our times is how to unleash each individual's distinctive, personal capacities to create prosperity. (p. 30)

9 MARKETS INFLUENCE and are influenced by the moral character of culture. Put simply, markets and culture matter. (p. 38)

10 TRADE IN IDEAS AND PRODUCTS and the movement of people are leading the way to a more global and integrated yet complex technological civilization. The world's operating system is in effect being written today. (p. 44)

11 AS WE MOVE THROUGH this global economic transition, a new Schumpeterian cycle of "creative destruction" and intense entrepreneurial competition and repositioning is sweeping through the world like a tornado. (p. 46)

12 THE PROSPECTS FOR CIVILITY are grounded in notions of human flourishing and conditioned on the premise that private, public, and social sectors each have something unique to provide the future. (p. 51)

13 THE WORLD IS NOW AKIN to a series of local area networks that form a cybernetic wide area network, accessible through the World Wide Web. Being outside the loop is to be cut off from the forces shaping the future. (p. 55)

14 THE HUMANITIES NEED TO BEFRIEND technological change and tame its darker side. Technology advances the prospects for human flourishing, empowers individual learning and innovation, and places learning at the core of economics; the humanities comprehend and record that fact, including the all-important human dimensions. (p. 57)

15 THE HUMANITIES need to be rethought to become the keystone to hold together the converging forces of globalization, technology, the explosion of knowledge, and the interaction of different cultures and religions. (p. 59)

16 WE MUST RECOGNIZE that victimhood is an intellectual dead-end. Victimhood as a critical and practical model paralyzes action and hope for some future good. (p. 81)

17 HUMAN BEINGS, in distinction from physical, biotic, and psychical entities, function as active agents in the entire range of fundamental dimensions—they think; they speak; and they believe. (p. 98)

18 AS MORAL ANIMALS, humans are inescapably interested in and guided by normative cultural orders that specify what is good, right, true, beautiful, worthy, noble, and just in life and what is not. (p. 98)

19 JUST AS LIBERTY, leadership, and happiness all depend on a well-developed self-regulating system of character, so creative intellectual and artistic work requires self-delineation and regulation. (p. 118)

20 THE INTEGRATED KNOWLEDGE ECONOMY of global proportions is free of the conflicts and shackles of the past. It is becoming more and more boundaryless. (p. 123)

21 AS GLOBAL DYNAMICS in economics, knowledge, and culture become increasingly powerful, a complementary power develops for localities that understand their role in the global order. Ironically, globalization results in an enlarged value for the local. (p. 125)

22 HUMANITIES-RICH COMMUNITIES that succeed in linking leadership, education, and cultural assets are more competitive and offer the prospect of a greater state of well-being and wellness for citizens. (p. 125)

23 CULTIVATING THE POTENTIAL for enlightened and responsible leadership appropriate to the new context of action means envisioning and designing curricula for a diverse global leadership. (p. 131)

24 THE STATE ALONE is no longer able or willing to fund the arts and humanities. Publics, as customers, are being asked to pay for services and goods on a contributory basis or in competitive, real markets. (p. 137)

25 THE HUMANITIES must be reengaged with intellectual renewal and reengagement with science, the arts, and religion in a constructive effort to envision and articulate a positive vision of a future of human prosperity and flourishing. (p. 138)

26 IN A GLOBALLY ROBUST knowledge economy driven by innovation, the not-for-profit sector needs to be rethought, and the humanities should play a critical role in helping to define both purpose and strategies. (p. 143)

27 LEADERS IN THE PRIVATE SECTOR must articulate the larger humanistic goals of commerce, and leaders in the social sector and humanities must come to understand the practical methods and rationales of knowledge-based economics. (p. 149)

28 **I**F PERSONAL HAPPINESS consists of well-fitted energies of individual character, social happiness, or justice, consists of well-fitted arrangements of a differentiated society and the skills and actions made possible through the humanistic mechanisms of finance and money. (p. 149)

29 **I**N THE PAST DECADE, the plethora of new laws, rules, and practices have made all organizations more accountable. The spread of higher standards for governance is laudable, worldwide. (p. 151)

30 **T**HE FUTURE OF DEMOCRACY and civil society depends on the success of corporations as key structures through which people freely associate and work together in a highly diversified and productive society. Corporate organization—in the for-profit and nonprofit sectors—is the primary organizational structure to create free and diverse societies. (p. 178)

31 **T**HE PUBLIC HUMANITIES are a critical source of spiritual, human, and social capital. The adage that societies with an abundance of social capital are healthier, more democratic, and more prosperous is proven. (p. 182)

32 **T**HERE IS AN URGENT CRY for humaneness, civility, and a restored sense that humans and the cultures they form and interact in should be rooted in a theory of development anchored not only in ever-growing material wealth, necessary as that may be, but also in a philosophy of human flourishing. (p. 184)

33 PRACTICAL PEOPLE may disagree about virtue or which virtues to exalt, but it is the humanities as the keeper of wisdom and personal narrative that allow and encourage such dialogue and contain it in the public sphere. (p. 184)

34 IF THE HUMANITIES are to flourish and regain their rightful place in public life, thereby influencing public discourse for the good, they must be based in a philosophy of the good. (p. 189)

35 MORE THAN EVER in a global, complex, and technological setting, and on a lonely planet, we seek wisdom, a dialogue grounded in the good that the humanities were created to foster and to sustain. Only then can we renew culture. (p. 190)

36 AS THE WELLSPRING of civic-mindedness, the humanities will achieve their intended purpose when they help to build more and lasting human, social, and spiritual capital. (p. 191)

Index

The Spiritual Enterprise Institute

It is the mission of the Spiritual Enterprise Institute (SEI) to function as a multidisciplinary center dedicated to exploring, analyzing and educating about the phenomenon of spiritual enterprise, entrepreneurship and capital in the global economy. SEI functions as a catalyst, bringing together academic, policy, business and religious leaders in order to develop a greater understanding of spiritual values across faiths, and their resulting impact on economic life, including communities, schools, education, productivity and growth.

An Agenda for Exploration and Development

SEI sponsors programs with the intent of stimulating research and products related to Spiritual Enterprise. Further, the Institute develops projects based on research that has a clear purpose and that will have significant strategic impact on the fields of science, business, public policy, religion, and culture overall.

SEI's Activities

- **Research** SEI undertakes and encourages research, polls and surveys on the phenomenon of spiritual enterprise and entrepreneurship worldwide through partnerships with universities, foundations, think tanks, and corporations and on its own accord.

- **Curriculum** SEI encourages faculty to consider appropriate ways to incorporate spiritual capital and globalization perspectives in the courses they teach and research they undertake. SEI also works with business schools to develop materials appropriate to integrate it into existing courses.

- **Conferences** SEI sponsors seminars, forums, roundtables and larger conferences to which academic, corporate, political, social sector and other leaders from around the world come to discuss, learn and share perspectives.

- **Lectures** SEI sponsors an annual series of lectures by nationally and internationally known leaders in academia, business and public policy.

- **Executive and Distance Education** SEI provides Executive Education programs in the area of Spiritual Entrepreneurship and Spiritual Capital.

- **Awards** SEI offers a number of global Prizes and Awards to luminaries and exemplars in the field of Spiritual Enterprise from the private, public and social sectors.

http://www.spiritualenterprise.org

About M & M Scrivener Press

———◆———

M & M Scrivener Press is a publishing house
devoted solely to issues dealing with
contemporary culture in the broad sense.
Over time, we will examine
ideas which impact our political and
cultural institutions as well as profit and
nonprofit organizations. With the world in a
continuous state of change, our series will
document and explore these changes and the
conflicts surrounding them.

Also available

Business and Religion
A Clash of Civilizations?

The contributors to this anthology comprise scholars, religious
and business leaders. They address the following questions:

- Is a purely secular business ethics irremediably
  deficient?
- Does a substantive business ethic require a religious and spiritual framework?
- To what extent does current business practice
  reflect a spiritual dimension?
- What are the various religious traditions' perspectives on the ethics of commerce?
- Can the various religious traditions generate a
  non-adversarial, consistent, and coherent business ethic?
- Is there a role for religion and spirituality in a
  global and postmodern business world?

Http://www.mmscrivenerpress.com